A THOUSAND WORDS

HEALING THROUGH ART FOR PEOPLE
WITH DEVELOPMENTAL DISABILITIES

Cindy Caprio-Orsini

Diverse City Press Inc. (La Presse Divers Cité Inc.)
BM 272, 33 des Floralies
Eastman, Québec
J0E 1P0   514-297-3080

Caprio-Orsini, Cynthia

A thousand words: Healing through art for people with
developmental disabilities

1. Developmental Disabilities
2. Trauma / Abuse
3. Therapy

ISBN 1-896230-07-5

LITHO CANADA   **Métrolitho** Sherbrooke (Québec)

A thoughtful and enlightening primer on the creative arts therapies. Excellent for those dedicated to healing and enriching the lives of those with developmental disabilities.
Marcia Herden, Psy.D., Clinical Psychologist

A THOUSAND WORDS makes a valuable contribution to the growing literature on therapy and counselling of those with developmental disabilities. The book illustrates art therapy makes a strong case for professionals expanding their repertoire of verbal therapies to include other modalities. The pervasiveness of life trauma of people with developmental disabilities demands we develop skills to meet the needs of *all* people with developmental disabilities. A refreshing, validating book. A must for those who serve people with developmental disabilities. *Sheila Mansell, Abuse and Disability Project*

Caprio-Orsini's work introduces a broad spectrum of therapeutic tools in working with people with disabilities who have been traumatized. Since encountering her work, I have successfully adapted her approaches into therapeutic practice. Her style of presentation allows one to readily understand her point and clearly respect her expertise. *Angie Nethercott, Coordinator York Sexuality Clinic*

I loved this book! Starting with the opening paragraph, Caprio-Orsini takes the reader on a journey from pain through to healing. We all know the amount of trauma that so many people with disabilities have experienced, Cindy offers a 'how-to' of hope. The first time I heard Cindy speak I knew I was listening to a gifted therapist whose compassion equalled her skill. Her teachings and her writings have increased my skill. I owe her much thanks for helping me serve better. *Dave Hingsburger, Consultant / Therapist*

This book is dedicated to all the people who were courageous enough to share their art work in order to help others understand the potential effects of abuse. It is dedicated to all the people that I have encountered in my work as an art therapist. They are the real teachers. Their art work speaks for itself. A picture is worth a thousand words.

To my wonderful, patient, and generous husband who has put up with me while working on this book. His encouragement, technical support and hugs were desperately needed.

To my lucky stars for being in the right place at the right time. I had just finished hearing Dave Hingsburger give a keynote lecture. I was impressed. My presentation followed. Dave walked in and sat down. I began to sweat. When he approached me at the end I braced myself for the worst. To my surprise he said, "Would you consider writing a book?" I thought he was joking. Later he called and said that he was excited, he had used one of the art techniques from my lecture and it worked. The person he was working with, for the first time began to express himself through drawing. He was very serious about the book. I am grateful our paths crossed. You have been an inspiration to me.

To my colleague, Marcia Herden, for her friendship, professional guidance, editing and constant support. I could not have done this without you. You were there for some very difficult times throughout the making of this book.

To my business partner, Jeff Schumacher, co-founder of The Forum: Advancement of Trauma Education, who has been an empathic friend (listening to my neurotic concerns) and has helped to make dreams come true.

And finally to my parents and siblings. The love that we share in our family was the catalyst for this book. Because of you I have been able to pass that on to others. It is a gift for which I am forever grateful. Thank you!

A Thousand Words
Preface: A Note From the Author

Trauma is devastating. What is even more devastating is never being given the chance to heal from the trauma. Yet it happens every day. Why? Even in an era of "progressive mental health treatment" there are an astounding number of people who believe that those with limited intellectual capacities, minimal verbal communication, or a disability are not able to benefit from trauma therapy. Better and easier to keep them medicated or preoccupied with simple tasks (tasks that even a rat could perform). Better for whom? Easier maybe, for those who say they care for them on a daily basis. Easier maybe for the agency providing services with minimal staff. Easier maybe, for those who provide funding.

Placating, distracting and denial only work for a short period of time. What about the human being who suffers on a daily basis as she remembers the horrors of ritual rape as part of her bed time routine? She now spends most of her time layered in clothing, terrified of the night, and unable to maintain relationships. What about the young man who constantly has flashbacks of sadistic beatings at the hands of his mother and boyfriends, then being passed around like a party favor for their sexual pleasures? He now has committed a number of sexual crimes and is physically violent toward others. No longer is it easier or better to ignore these problems. Medication and menial tasks do not take away the core problem. Trauma does not disappear just because someone is disabled. All human beings deserve the respect, dignity and opportunity to heal from trauma.

This book encourages the use of creative art techniques. It is for those who have difficulty orally communicating and expressing themselves as a result of a disability and/or trauma. Creative art making offers an avenue to safely communicate emotions. It helps to resolve problems such as sexual, physical, and emotional trauma. It allows one to express and begin making sense of difficult emotions. Art making provides situations where one can create something beautiful and powerful out of the ugliness of trauma. This book provides examples of art work, techniques and case studies that illustrate the potentials of creating and communicating through art. It is for professionals working with people who are developmentally disabled, language impaired, or for those who are just tired of traditional verbal approaches to therapy. The art work in this book is primarily done by individuals who are disabled, however I have selected some pieces from people without disabilities because their art work poignantly illustrates specific points.

One area that I struggled with throughout this book was the wording for the group of people that I have chosen to discuss. I oppose labeling people for their differences and see all people with abilities, not disabilities. Despite my convictions, I was unable to clearly discuss specific differences without referring to descriptive labels. When possible, I prefer to use the word PEOPLE, because that is who we all are. People with disabilities even disagree on the best term to use when describing them. I have found the best way to handle describing disabilities is to ask the person what is their personal preference. It does not have to be complicated because the bottom line is respecting individual differences. When I am caught up in the bizarre bureaucracy of labeling I am reminded (and usually figuratively) of a special person who has one simple desire for the universe. She says, "If only everyone could see people for who they are instead of who they are not. Below every label we are all the same. Human beings." This may not be an exact quotation but it certainly is the essence of an important message that we can all learn from.

This book is not intended to provide the reader with enough information to implement art therapy techniques. Practicing art therapy requires professional training and registration from the American Art Therapy Association. The information in this book is not based on any hard data and I have deliberately avoided professional jargon. The book does offer basic information about the effects of trauma, about the art therapy process, and some creative techniques to help in the healing process. It is written mainly for mental health providers who work with people who are language impaired and are seeking approaches to help them explore trauma related issues. It is hoped that this book will encourage practitioners to seek diverse modalities to enable people with disabilities to express themselves and potentially heal from trauma. As I stress throughout this book, there is no limit to creativity or who can create. The art experience can provide a magical alternative to spoken communication. It may result in externalizing, often for the first time, internal worlds that may otherwise never be discovered.

Contents

Introduction

It was my first day at a new job. I was excited. It was a chance to follow my dream. I would be using my love for art and working with people who would be eager to discover the possibilities of art. Naive? Yes! And a little arrogant as well. I pushed back the door of the room anticipating nothing but the best. I gasped! There in front of me was a disarray of paint by number kits, plastic molds for ceramics, and mounds of ancient newsprint paper that crumbled to the touch. This was a nightmare. Not the dream I had anticipated. Fortunately, I was able to rewrite this script and turn the nightmare into a manageable situation.

As the director at a camp for children with developmental disabilities, I had decided to incorporate the concept of creativity. Then came the art-in-a-box nightmare. I momentarily reconsidered cutting lawns for a living. I could somehow find a way to be creative with a lawn mower. I tried to be rational. I asked myself, wouldn't it be easier to just agree with the program? What right did I have to come in and expect it to be done differently? I started to go through the art materials (if you could call them that). The lawn mowing job started to look better and better. But, I did not give up. Instead, I went to my supervisor with a list of new art supplies and a proposal for a project. My persistence paid off, for the most part. The 20 easels and $5,000 kiln were turned downed (you might as well go for it all) but all the other essential supplies were approved.

Then came the next of many challenges. This was getting the children to use materials that were not the paint by number type. I approached this challenge by getting them involved right from the start. This was a new concept to them as they were accustomed to being told what to do, not asked what they want to do. I asked and they looked at me, in silence, as if I were from

1

outer space. Finally, after they realized I was serious and from Earth, we were able to organize an art project to work on throughout the course of the summer. Two things immediately became evident to onlookers. First, the project did not involve stencils and precut materials. Spontaneous creativity was introduced, encouraged and being used. Secondly, the children were involved in the entire process. This was met with some skepticism by staff. It was foreign to them when working with people who are developmentally disabled. After all, didn't I ever hear of the easy "premade-all-you-have-to-do-is-glue-it-together" art projects that can be ordered from the catalogs? They did not expect the children to be able to follow through with such an unstructured creative project. Being persistent (others have labeled this quality of mine as stubborn), I ignored this and proceeded with my plan.

My plan, however, included MY preconceived idea of how the finished product would look. I quickly realized my mistake and was reminded that this was not MY project but the children's. I did not need to prove anything to the suspicious staff or to myself. The children were already engrossed in the project and thoroughly enjoying the indulgence of immersing themselves in the art materials. This is when I first started to believe that the beauty of art is the process, not the product. I learned to let go of embedded messages from strict art teachers who had emphasized that the product is most important in art. Realizing this rigidity allowed me to see that the art making process needs to be enjoyed, and without the judgment of others who think they may know what is best.

It was exhilarating to observe the children be involved in the creative process. At first there were insecurities with the new paints and clay. They never had been presented with the opportunity to "create" without some sort of prefabricated materials. By offering them high quality materials they naturally began believing in themselves. The children did not need rigid structures and guidelines. They became increasingly comfortable with their freedom of expression. The result? A magnificent three dimensional sculpture and painted mural and a room full of extremely proud children. A Monet masterpiece it was not, but an original, fresh and powerful piece of art it was! This was the magic and power of art. A picture IS worth a thousand words.

This example illustrates the power that art exemplifies and what can be discovered in the creative process. Throughout this project I watched the children's self-esteem blossom. I recognized that emotions were being shared with less hesitancy and saw anxiety reduced in those who were tense and rigid. They worked together as a team, built confidence, and got to the heART of it. It was with this experience that I readily acknowledged the need and importance for creativity with people who are developmentally disabled. Just as importantly, I realized the need to educate the skeptics about the power of art and all the potential creativity can offer to those with disabilities. It was then that I decided to pursue an art therapy degree.

While working on my degree in art therapy I had the fortunate opportunity to work with an art therapist who shared my passion for creative art making and working with people who are developmentally disabled. My year interning with art educator and art therapist David Henley was invaluable. I am forever grateful for all that he taught me. The need for creative art making with those who are disabled was validated by this experience. One would only have to enter the art room that David had set up to view the many possibilities. My passion for art flourished in his room. The impact of the rich and expressive images that were proudly displayed was powerfully contagious!

Over time I became increasingly interested in working with trauma survivors partly due to my own personal encounters with loss and trauma. Art helped me survive through some very difficult times. I was also naturally drawn to working with people who are disabled. So I integrated these two interests with art therapy. I found that many people who are disabled have been severely abused and traumatized. Their traumas stem from physical, emotional, and sexual abuse. It also involves abuse from the very systems that were supposed to help them. For example, agencies that set "goals" they felt would be best for the client. Personally, I feel being forced to achieve a goal that is decided on by others is abusive. Based on all this, it was obvious to me that people with disablities do suffer from abuse. They also deserve the opportunity to heal from trauma. Nevertheless, I still encountered resistance from professionals in the agencies I worked. I believe this resistance came from the belief that the existence of trauma or abuse with someone who is disabled never occurs. Their opposition may have stemmed from the skepticism that therapy of any kind could be beneficial for people with developmental disablities, especially psychotherapy. I found myself trying to convince the skeptics through limited available research. I even presented written case examples. It took some time to realize that this was not a productive approach. I was beginning to deplete my energy. However, I did not give up. I redirected my energy by letting the art speak for itself. Slowly, those who originally doubted the occurrence of sexual abuse and trauma among people with disabilities began to visually see the reality of this tragedy through the art work. The healing powers of art for people with disablities clearly became evident. The art spoke for itself. Pictures are worth a thousand words.

Trauma and those with Developmental Disabilities

I received a phone call from a local agency. They wanted me to meet with a young man who had limited verbal skills and was having behavioral problems at his residential facility. The staff was frustrated and did not know what to do with Mick. They reported that he spent many hours in the bathroom washing himself obsessively after using the toilet. He became enraged when staff tried to intervene. They did not understand why Mick was doing this. He was unable (or unwilling?) to tell them why. According to staff there were other "problems" as well. He became furious when given oatmeal for breakfast. Mick refused to remove his coat even on the hottest summer days.

I agreed to see him. Mick and I quickly established a trusting relationship as he was thrilled with the abundant array of art materials. It did not take long before Mick began to spontaneously use the art materials as a way to communicate with me. Although I suspected a history of abuse based on his reported behaviors, it was validated through his art work. He drew many pictures of bathrooms filled with the color red. When asked about this he was able to further draw pictures that illustrated violent attacks between himself and another man. Later in therapy Mick explained the oatmeal aversion, through his art. He was forced to eat this for every meal, every day. No wonder he did not want to eat oatmeal!

When I explained to staff that these behaviors were related to past abuse, it was met with resistance. It did not matter to them what had happened to Mick in the past. There was a program to follow and he needed to follow it. Eventually they did allow him to forego the oatmeal. We worked on reducing time in the bathroom. I pointed out to staff that wearing a coat in the summer was not hurting him (when he got hot enough he did remove it). Begrudgingly, staff worked with me, but I always sensed that they did not understand the effects of severe abuse.

Post Traumatic Stress Disorder (PTSD) is commonly experienced by people who have been severely traumatized. It is disturbing to me that even today people in the mental health profession still do not believe that someone with a developmental disability can suffer from PTSD. I know of one psychiatrist who once said about a young man with developmental disabilities, "He isn't experiencing PTSD. He just has a bad brain." Who has a bad brain?

Symptoms of PTSD are commonly experienced by people with developmental disabilities who have suffered from abuse. As defined by the DSM-IV, the traumatic event is reexperienced in a number of different ways. Mick, for example, was acting or feeling as if the traumatic event was still happening and exhibited intense emotional distress at being exposed to situations that resembled the traumatic event. These two examples of the criteria that are part of the PTSD diagnosis listed in the DSM-IV. Signs that a person may be suffering from PTSD are:

- efforts to avoid thoughts, feelings, or conversations associated with the trauma
- efforts to avoid activities, places, or people that bring back memories of the trauma
- inability to remember an important aspect of the trauma
- notably less interest or participation in significant activities
- feeling detached or removed from others
- unable to experience a range of feelings
- sense of a shortened future
- difficulty falling or staying asleep

- irritability or outbursts of anger
- difficulty concentrating
- increased level of awareness or alertness
- exaggerated startle response.

I am sure the above symptoms may be recognizable or familiar. This is not a complete list. The DSM-IV describes PTSD in further detail and should be referred to if you suspect someone may be experiencing this.

People do not want to believe that abuse exists and even fewer people want to admit that it exists among those who are developmentally disabled. This disbelief appears to exist for a variety of reasons. Doubt may originate from denial, a personal abuse history, or perhaps having been a perpetrator. Despite this disbelief the reality is that people with disabilities are more vulnerable to incest, trauma and sexual abuse because they are less able to protect themselves and less likely to receive adequate social services.

Why are people with disabilities abused? Children and adults who do not have full physical or emotional capacities are easy targets because of their vulnerabilities. From a young age, disabled children are taught to rely upon and submit to their caregivers. By adolescence they have usually learned that cooperation gains them a small measure of independence and perhaps even survival. What they have not learned is asser-tiveness, self-protective skills, or adequate sex education. It is what people with developmental disabilities are **not** educated about that leads to being easily intimidated, confused, and silenced. What they have not learned leads to abuse or trauma. Trauma is defined as an emotional, physical or sexual shock that creates substantial and lasting damage to the psychological and often physical development of the individual.

All children are vulnerable to abuse because of the tremendous difference in power that exists between them and adults. The risk for abuse is greater when there is dependency on an adult. People who are disabled are more dependent on adults for their everyday needs. It is estimated that children with disabilities are four to ten times more vulnerable to sexual abuse than their non-disabled peers (Tobin, 1992). Another estimate suggests that a child with a disability is at least one and a half times more likely to be abused. This estimate depends on the definition of abuse and if multiple victimizations are considered. It could be as high as five times greater (Sobsey, 1992). These vulnerabilities to sexual abuse may be due to total dependence on caregivers and other adults, isolation, low self-esteem, blurred boundaries with regard to their body, and forced compliance. In addition, public disbelief that leads to denial increases the potential for becoming vulnerable.

Therapeutic Treatment Approaches

Not all therapists can work with everyone (although some would like to believe they can). I for one thought that I should and could be able to work with all kinds of people. I was invincible. I was wrong! I eventually had to come to grips with the fact that I had limitations. I just could not (and did not have to) work with everyone, especially with people that might stir up something that may not be entirely put to rest for me.

To work therapeutically with people who are developmentally disabled it is necessary to have a broad background in special education and disabilities. The therapist must be comfortable interacting with a person who is developmentally disabled in an accepting and non-judgemental manner. The most important thing that I have learned is that we are working with human beings, first and foremost. Titles and labels only inhibit the therapeutic process. People with disabilities are human beings, not labels. If a therapist can recognize this then therapy will most likely to naturally occur.

While working on this book I received a very moving letter from the parents of Jason, a delightful young man whom I had the pleasure of working with for a few years. Jason was an amazingly talented artist (Figure 1). An excerpt from the letter emphasizes the point that I refer to above. It states, "....We feel that the general public should be made more aware of **abilities**, rather than constantly focusing on `disabilities´. We are quite proud of Jason. As Helen Keller said, `A person who is severely impaired never knows his hidden resources of strength until he is treated like a human being and encouraged to share his own life.´ We want people to know Jason and share his life." (The Vetra's, 1995)

Jason's artistic ability was discovered because someone took the time to treat him as a human being and uncovered his hidden resources of strength. Jason is fortunate. He has supportive and nurturing parents. He has always been encouraged to use the creative arts to communicate. Many people that have disabilities are never given this opportunity.

A therapist may need to spend time with a person who is disabled outside the confines of the office. What occurs in the office is important, but what goes on

Figure 1   *Jason's acrylic painting.*

outside the office is their reality. It will increase awareness of the person's potential in many areas, as well as their everyday struggles. Being out in the community with a person who is physically or developmentally challenged is an eye opening experience. It clearly illustrates society's ignorance with regard to disabilities. It also acknowledges how what we take for granted could become a laborious situation for someone with a disability. Just getting into a store can become an exhausting experience. Handicapped parking is often ignored. Ramps are frequently blocked by ignorant people. Rude comments are made within earshot. These folks are often retraumatized on a daily basis. Personal dignity and respect can become virtually nonexistent due to how our society behaves.

Margaret is a good therapist. She uses all the right therapeutic terminology. Her office is neat and comfortable. She has therapeutic goals that she adheres to according to her professional standards. She is well respected in the community and has been very successful with the clients she has served.However, she would never cut it with a person who needed flexibility, creativity, and genuine compassion. She could not work with a person who needed to sit on the floor or hide under the table because that is all they ever knew. She could not work with a person who needed to throw clay against a board to release their anger (too messy!). She could not work with someone who required more than just therapeutic jargon.

Flexibility and creativity are essential qualities for the therapist who works with someone who is disabled and has been traumatized. Flexibility is needed in order to adapt and change therapy plans as needed. One may need to be willing to plop down on the floor and facilitate a session. It is helpful to individualize counseling techniques to meet the needs of the person and be willing to change techniques as needed throughout the course of therapy. Creativity is necessary because therapy materials must often be implemented in innovative ways. For example, in order to create art a person who is physically challenged may need special tools or accommodations to feel safe and secure in the therapy setting. Art materials may require adaptations to help facilitate expression.

Communication with people who are developmentally disabled will require that the therapist learn how they use expressive language. Family, caseworkers, agency staff, or any person who has spent significant time with the person will be able to teach about their specific body language and personal expressions. Assessing receptive language is also important. Does this person understand what I am saying? Direct communication is the best approach. Depending on the person's language it may be necessary to use simpler sentences and words. Pictures, drawings, or photos can be referred to if receptive language is limited.

Visible signs of progress of a person who has been abused and is developmentally disabled are often minimal. They occur only after long term interventions. For instance, an initial goal may be to appropriately use the art materials to visually express a feeling. This is an unrealistic goal if the person never used art materials before. What if they were never allowed to express feelings? A more realistic goal would be to forget the complexity of it and simplify it to address just one aspect. Perhaps the goal would be to play with art materials. This may take many months of hand-over-hand techniques to accomplish this if the person never used art materials in the past. The therapist may need to assist the person directly by showing them what the materials can do before they even attempt to express a feeling. This can be demonstrated, with their permission, by placing your hand over theirs and making marks on the paper.

11

At times the therapist may need to be aware of her counter-transference or responses she may have to the person with whom she is working. If the therapist is not flexible or sets unrealistic goals then frustration is inevitable. Goals are reached at a much slower pace with the person who is developmentally disabled. It is important to take notice of the less obvious. For example, every time I meet with someone for a session, gains are made. These gains may not meet state requirements but they are personal achievements for the client. If all they remember is being punished for doing anything, then just by having the courage to come in and pick up a marker is an achievement. I find that it is more important to focus on the person, rather than the goals.

The nature and principles of therapeutic methods used with people who have been traumatized and are developmentally disabled do not differ from those who are not disabled. Nevertheless, the implementation may differ. It does involve a basic understanding by the mental health provider of specific and various disabilities and the impact on communication, social, emotional, and behavioral development. Psychotherapy can help people who are disabled to understand and resolve their difficulties. This involves the therapist actively offering advice, encouraging mutual discussion, and providing creative outlets. Traditional psychotherapy it is not. Freud might disapprove. Yet this type of interactive therapy can help to achieve maturity, autonomy, reestablish trust and develop basic skills in living.

Goals in Therapy

Goals in therapy when working with those who are disabled are similar to the goals when working with any person who has been traumatized. Treatment, however, requires tailoring to meet individual needs, based on the uniqueness of each person. Regardless of the severity of the disability, at some point the goal is to reestablish a sense of trust and safety. It is important to be accepting and consistent in order to help the person feel safe and be able to build trust. Attention to the smallest detail is essential. What may appear insignificant to you may be very significant to someone who has never felt safe. For example, I had been working with a young woman, Jill, for about a year. Staff from her group home brought her to treatment every week. They always waited for her. One day they said they were going to run an errand and would return before the end of the session. Jill and I went into my office. I noticed that Jill was unusually agitated. She was pacing in front of the window. Normally she went right to the art materials. It finally hit me. Jill was concerned that her ride would not return. I had not paid attention to this detail. Of course this was anxiety provoking for her. Her mother often left her for days at a time as a young child. Jill did not trust that they would return for her. I mistakenly overlooked the significance of staff waiting for her while she was in session. This example reminds us that the road to recovery from trauma is long. Patience, stability, and consistency on the part of the therapist are imperative.

Various therapeutic interventions will be needed to help achieve the goals of therapy. Play and art therapies are especially helpful for those who have speech and language impairments. This type of therapeutic intervention may be an adjunct to primary therapy, or it may be more appropriate as the primary mode. Instructive techniques may be needed to teach concepts about human sexuality or to develop affective vocabulary in order to help express feelings more accurately. Reality testing will be helpful to assist the person in making reality-based decisions. Other techniques that may help the client reach specific goals in therapy might include behavioral contracting, psychodrama and role playing, or other expressive therapies.

In my work as an art therapist with people who are

developmentally disabled, I focus on goals based on individual needs. These goals are developed **with** the person, not **for** the person. I find that goals may not always be the focus of sessions. Being purely human, with no agenda, may be the most helpful. It is never my agenda, it is always their agenda. I have found that the modality of art therapy helps to work through problems in a more helpful manner than traditional psychotherapy with people who are developmentally disabled. It allows the person with a language impairment a safe, creative, and visual way to communicate thoughts and feelings.

People who have been traumatized often feel that what they have endured is their fault. They experience tremendous guilt and have difficulty trusting peers, adults, and themselves. In therapy, the goal is to help alleviate the guilt engendered by the abuse and restore the ability to trust people again. Teaching about abuse will assist in developing an understanding about what has happened to them. It will help to decrease feelings often described as being "damaged goods". When teaching about abuse it is important to include information about physical, sexual and emotional abuse at the appropriate developmental level. There are many books available that provide information about abuse (see bibliography).

Another goal in the therapeutic process is to encourage appropriate expression of feelings, primarily anger. The therapist may need to teach the client how to express anger in productive ways. I have found that people with developmental disabilities who have been traumatized often express their anger through acting out behaviors. For example, they express their intense rage through fire setting, physical and sexual assaults of others, self injury, and other forms of destructive behavior. In the beginning of therapy, when dealing with anger, the level of rage that is unleashed may be intense for some clients. This is the result of

14

years of silencing and being on the receiving end of severe abuse. The development of affective vocabulary can help to widen the range of their emotional expressions. This aids in facilitating appropriate discharge of their internal chaos. People with developmental disabilities often have limited labels for feelings and emotions. Their repertoire may include only basic words such as happy, sad, and mad. The use of art therapy is helpful to visually illustrate various language concepts for emotions and to widen the range for expressing feelings.

Basic information concerning normal human sexuality and interpersonal relationships rarely is presented to a person with a developmental disability. This may be due to misconceptions that people with handicaps are asexual. It is therefore important to teach basic human sexuality since this area is often neglected. For example, proper sexuality is required to address human reproduction, contraception and safe sex, and sexual identity issues. To facilitate this goal, specific books that focus on these topics are readily available at age-appropriate levels. (Dave Hingsburger's books are highly recommended). Sexuality training may also be available in your area for this population.

Poor self-esteem and feelings of negative self-worth are commonly experienced by someone who has been traumatized. One goal will need to be focusing on improving self-esteem. This can occur through the teaching of assertiveness techniques to increase self-awareness and self-protection. Through role play and visual avenues such as art therapy, a person can learn how to recognize and exhibit their personal strengths and powers. Creating something completely on your own is just one way to build self-esteem.

The lack of respect that people have for those with disabilities is astounding. This certainly has been my experience when I spend time with my clients outside, or inside the building or waiting area. People will often talk directly to the non-disabled person about the person with the disability as if the person with the disability is invisible. What does this say to the person who is disabled? Our society claims that they are sensitive to the needs of people with disabilities. This kind of treatment can be abusive or at least extremely humiliating. One goal in therapy is to help the client to identify the difference between an abusive and a non-abusive situation. Being ignored is one example of an abusive situation. If this is all a person knows she may not view it as abusive. The development of a personal value system can help increase self-awareness and therefore promote awareness in others.

The disabled may experience depression as a result of abuse. Depression is often part of PTSD and needs to be treated. It will not spontaneously remit. This is a common misconception by some who feel that people with developmental disabilities are not capable of depression. Symptoms may include sleep disturbances, loss of appetite or compulsive eating, difficulties in concentration, perseveration, and suicidal thoughts. These symptoms may go unrecognized, as they are often difficult to detect. If there is any suspicion of depression a psychiatric evaluation is recommended. Medication may also be necessary at times.

These goals may not apply for all people that are being treated for abuse as goals will vary on an individual basis. There may be other goals that are not included here. This is only a brief overview of some of the more common issues that I focus on in art therapy sessions.

2

Beyond Basket Weaving

Definition of Art Therapy

"Art therapy? Oh, you mean like that handwriting analysis? What do you do, color and basket weave?" "What is art therapy?" is a common question art therapists are asked. Many people have never heard of art therapy. If they have they often confuse it with other disciplines in the health field, such as occupational therapy. Basket weaving would fall into the occupational therapy category. The simplest definition, and the essence of art therapy, is that it involves both creating art and therapy. Art is not limited to drawings and paintings and it is much more than handwriting analysis. It can include three dimensional work such as sculpture, wood working, and pottery. It may also incorporate movement, role play, puppetry, and the use of music. Art therapy encourages creativity. It is not just for children. The vehicles for expressing oneself creatively can be limitless and healing for all ages.

Art therapy with people who are developmentally disabled involves encouraging the exploration of personal problems, expressed through alternative communication methods. Creating art can help develop physical, emotional, behavioral, and learning skills through visual expression. Art therapy offers an opportunity for individuals to manipulate materials, as well as the environment, in which they create. This can provide a sense of being in control, a feeling that is often lacking for people who are disabled and those that have been traumatized. They can symbolically explore and organize meaning from a world that is often overwhelming. This may help reduce some of the confusion and frustration (Figure 2) that is experienced in their chaotic lives. I know for me that after a particularly bad day with numerous thoughts racing through my head, it is helpful to jot down or draw those thoughts. I feel more organized when they are put out there visually. I am the queen of sticky yellow papers with notes written to myself. As long as I don't forget where I put the yellow sticky paper I feel more at peace.

Figure 2   *Organizing a disturbing event.*

You walk into a bookstore looking for a cookbook. Some people do this, don't they? *(Take-out menus are much easier.)* Anyway, when you find the right section, would you be more apt to purchase a cookbook with a recipe scrawled across the cover, or the one with a delicious, mouth watering you-can-almost-taste-it image of the completed recipe? If you thought the former I am sure **this** book makes no sense. Visual images usually have more impact than words.

Art is a visual language that transcends spoken or written words. With individuals who, for whatever reason, have difficulty understanding language or making themselves understood, the first goal must be widening the range of communication. In order to feel in control one must have a way to communicate and be understood. Language equals power, and art is extremely powerful (Figure 3). Image making is a powerful way of eliciting painful and frightening pictures from within. Art making can be a direct way to express nightmares, fantasies, and other inner experiences that appear naturally in pictures rather than words. Art does not require language.

Art therapy is a treatment modality that has a unique role in healing from trauma. It provides a safe place to non-verbally explore trauma-related issues. Art therapy supports the development of increased egostrength and positive self-

Figure 3   *Art is a language of its own.*

esteem, both which are damaged by abuse. This in turn fosters strengthening the individual's sense of personal boundaries. For people who are disabled these boundaries are frequently blurred by constant intrusions on their bodies by caregivers. Privacy is not something they are generally given. Abuse further violates physical boundaries.

Art work helps to assist in visually identifying primary issues that may not appear in overt behavior (Figure 4). Artwork may express an individual's developmental level and cognitive functioning. Additionally, art making provides an arena for the expression of aggression, self-concept and other strong emotions.

As an art therapist it is important to know and understand who and what you are treating. Art therapy includes diagnostic assessment and treatment. Art therapist Judith Rubin points out in the article *Art Therapy: What It Is and What It Is Not*, that it is also important to know about art and making art. One must know what to do when someone is trying to attach an arm to a clay body. Just sticking it on will not work. You would end up with an armless person once the clay dried and one very upset client, unless the client intended to create an armless figure. The art therapist must understand both the creative process and the nature of symbols, as well as form and content. Rubin states that the art therapist needs to be knowledgeable about herself (this

Figure 4   *Feelings about family.*

means more than just what your favorite movie is) as well as others with regard to development, psychodynamics, and interpersonal relations. Finally, it is important to know about the treatment relationship and the underlying mechanisms that help others to change and grow (Rubin, 1984).

The practice of art therapy requires extensive training. Art therapists who have met educational, professional and ethical standards specified by the American Art Therapy Association (AATA) are eligible to become Registered Art Therapists (A.T.R.) once criteria is met. Recently Board Certification (BC) has become available for A.T.R.'s. This is acquired through a certification exam.

Creative Art Making: It IS for everyone!

If you are one of those people who struggle with a stick figure drawing, then you may be having some trouble with this subtitle.

It is true. We are all capable of creative art making. It may require a few corrective experiences if your elementary art teacher was a tyrant, never complimenting your efforts. But you can move beyond stick figure drawings **and** have people actually recognize what you are drawing. Creativity is for everyone.

Traditionally people believe that those who are disabled are not capable of spontaneous creative art because of their concrete thinking process. Yet I constantly witness how far from reality this belief is. For example, a brilliant young woman who is visually impaired eloquently sculpts out of clay images that represent her feelings associated with past abuse. Her art work is created in a purely spontaneous manner (no paint by number for her!). This certainly provides evidence that she is capable of creating art (Figure 5). There may be times when a person appears un-interested in making art. However, if someone is struggling with the art materials and is not interacting with them, it may be that they were deprived of making art, or perhaps had a critical art teacher. It is the art therapist's challenge to help find a way for that person to develop the desire to create.

Figure 5   *Past abuse sculpted in clay.*

A number of people who are developmentally disabled are deficient in language development. The art therapist is adept at facilitating nonverbal approaches so this does not present a considerable problem for treating people with developmental disabilities. What is nice about the art therapy process is that it lessens anxiety and sense of failure. People who are disabled may feel inadequate when presented with tasks that interfere with their intellectual and communication deficits. With art therapy and creative expression they are encouraged to use the art materials and their creativity in whatever way they desire. There are no wrongs when being creative. Nevertheless, there may be negative messages or experiences related to making art that are deeply ingrained. By now you probably have figured it out with all the references to "bad" art teachers. I had an art teacher from Hell. She made me stand up in front of everyone and moo like a cow because I was chewing gum. Anyone caught chewing gum paid this price. As a seventh grader this was more than just humiliating. It left me with horrible memories and temporarily stifled my creative process. Luckily, I later had a wonderful art teacher who provided me with plenty of corrective experiences. I eventually went on to become an art teacher and art therapist.

The art therapist may need to help redefine the meaning of art. An important message that I continuously repeat is, "all art is beautiful, especially art that comes from within and is created solely by the person". I once witnessed an inappropriate and creativity-hindering intervention, one of many unfortunately. A staff person at a group home had removed a drawing from a client. The client had been intensely concentrating on his drawing. The staff person told the client that his drawing was not allowed. It graphically depicted two anatomically correct people engaged in a sexual activity. The drawing was hurting no one. What kind of message is this when someone is forbidden to draw something? I feel it is two-fold. The messages are that sex is bad, and that expressing oneself through art is unacceptable. It is crucial to accept all types of drawings, no matter what the content. All drawings are valid means of communication.

Challenges are plentiful when working with people who have been traumatized. A young man named Johnny who is deaf, blind, and developmentally disabled presented such a challenge. For Johnny, one of many things he had been deprived of was exposure to art materials. Unsure as to what to do with the art materials, he initially spent a significant amount of time isolating himself. Johnny rocked back and forth in his chair. Occasionally, he picked up a Craypa. Later he explored the Craypa by putting it in his mouth. It became clear that Johnny's first attempt at using the art materials would require an intervention.

I quietly drew next to him for a number of sessions. Eventually, to my surprise and delight he joined me. This then led to spontaneous use of the art materials. Johnny began to randomly make marks on the paper. Weeks went by while he feverishly filled paper after paper, indulging in the box of colorful Craypas.

Later he began to form simple geometric shapes. When he appeared comfortable with this, I gently encouraged him to add different shapes by using hand-over-hand techniques (Figure 6). I placed my hand on his, with his permission, and we explored many different shapes. Throughout the course of a year he began to exhibit an increased interest in people. He no longer rocked in his chair. He became part of the group.

Figure 6 *Initial drawing attempts.*

Johnny started to study people. He initiated contact with them by touching their faces. Then an amazing thing happened. Faces began to appear in his art work. Johnny did not stop here. He continued to embellish the face drawings

Figure 7   *Faces began to appear.*

(Figure 7). Soon full figures of people surfaced (Figure 8). In addition to his interest in people, he began to develop a desire to explore a different medium. Watercolor paints became his passion (Figure 9).

Over the course of two years Johnny had significantly changed. His original, often impoverished art work converted into rich and highly expressive pieces (Figure 10). What this case illustrates is that with encouragement and appropriate interventions people who are disabled can eloquently express themselves through art. Most importantly, as with Johnny, they are provided with an alternative to communicate, to express themselves, and nurture innate abilities.

I have repeatedly found that people

Figure 8   *Full figures emerged.*

Figure 9   *The discovery of watercolors paint.*

who are disabled unfortunately have limited opportunities to create art prefabricated materials, or they have been completely deprived of the art experience. They may need to be acquainted with the materials, helped to manipulate them, or given a special device to use them. It is important to evaluate the physical, mental, and emotional condition of the individual in order to provide the appropriate conditions for him to create to his fullest potential. This will require the therapist to use her own creativity to meet the challenge of offering those with disabilities the advantage of spontaneously creating art.

Providing people the experience to manipulate and work with art materials helps them to expand their sensory, perceptual, and motor skills. This can lead to an increased awareness of their surroundings and of themselves that can help to prevent further victimization and trauma. (Figure 11). They may develop self-worth, safety, and confidence,

Figure 10   *Combining new interests!*

25

while increasing visual organizational skills and releasing emotions. These personal gains can be generated through creative art experiences.

Creativity is important in the lives of all individuals. It is basically a universal form of communication. One can give form to feelings, ideas, values, and needs. Art can encompass every aspect of human feeling. It speaks to our private inner lives. Art encourages exploration and inventive behavior. People who are disabled are often discouraged from being inventive. "Tasks" usually focus on such things as setting the table the proper way. Who cares as long as you have utensils and a plate? Art also presents opportunities to work with others as equals. Remember, there are no wrongs in art. Even throwing the paint can have wonderful results. Jackson Pollock made millions doing this.

Figure 11   *Drawing of a safe surrounding.*

Art fosters independence in thinking and solutions. It provides opportunities for success and personal achievements. It offers a vast number of sensory, intellectual, social, and emotional experiences, some of which are impossible to get through other means. Art making is a way to think through and test concepts, strengths, and skills, through manipulation of materials. I could go on about the importance of art, but I think you have the picture by now.

Stick Figures and More

A. Developmental Phases of Art

Infants become toddlers. Toddlers grow into youths. We all progress from stage to stage along the developmental continuum. Some may remain at one phase much longer than others. I certainly know a number of people still in the

Figure 12   *Scribbling Stage*

rebellious adolescent stage. People who are developmentally disabled often are delayed in their growth. Some people regress in development depending on circumstances. We can all relate to times when we just wanted someone to take care of us. Development in artistic expression progresses in a similar manner.

I have found that the art work of people who are developmentally disabled is often misinterpreted. It is essential to understand developmental phases if one is to generally understand what is being communicated through art and why.

Figure 13   *Preschematic Stage*

27

Victor Lowenfeld, an art educator, described the different stages of the development of art. The art therapist or art educator knows these developmental phases of children's art in order to provide steps toward higher functioning. Basic knowledge of these phases is important for anyone doing art with others, or if you have young children of your own. It is very reassuring for me to know that when my son omits the mouth on his picture of mom that it's not about his negative feelings associated with my excessive talking. It is more about the developmental phase he is in with regard to his art work. Chart 1 outlines the various stages.

Chart 1

Lowenfeld's Developmental Phases of Art

STAGE	AGE	BRIEF DESCRIPTION
Scribbling Stage	2-4 years	Includes random, longitudinal, circular and naming of scribble
Preschematic Stage	4-7 years	Initial emergence of the human figure
Schematic Stage	7-9 years	First concept of space and base line
Dawning Realism	9-11 years	Stereotypes and self-consciousness appear
Pseudorealistic stage of reasoning	11-13 years	Art becomes more realistic

For detailed information on developmental phases of art refer to Victor Lowenfeld: *Creative and Mental Growth* (1961)

Each developmental stage contains different areas and characteristics that can be identified in children's art work. The therapist looks for these areas to help identify the stage in which a person may be functioning. The areas in each stage that one looks at are: characteristics, human figures, space, color, and design (Lowenfeld, 1961). Examples of each stage are illustrated in Figures 12 through 16.

Figure 14   *Schematic Stage*

People who are developmentally disabled are often arrested at an earlier drawing phase. Moving beyond this stage varies, depending on the circumstances of this arrested development. Traumatization often causes suspension in development, usually at the age when the trauma occurred. It may also be due to environmental or emotional deprivation. Abuse of most types frequently includes neglect. This interferes with and deprives the child of normal experiences that involve art making. In these circumstances the potential for developmental progress in drawing is not obtained. The answer is not complex.

Figure 15   *Stage of Drawing Realism.*

All that may be needed is encouragement and a big box of pastels.

B. Trauma in Art Development

Figure 16   *Pseudorealistic Reasoning*

It is a confusing world out there. Television commercials tell us we need to diet. Magazine articles say we are not eating right. Mom says we are too thin. No wonder so many people suffer from eating disorders and have distorted body images. This is without the added complexities of abuse and developmental disabilities. People who are developmentally disabled are often confused about their bodies, in part due to limited sex education. Abuse can further create confusion about body image. The concept of space may be effected in response to trauma. The result in the art work may be a distorted image of the human figure. For example, a self-portrait may be drawn unusually small or may contain merged body parts (Figure 17). Prior to the abuse, a drawing of oneself may have covered the entire piece of paper, or been drawn with clear and separate

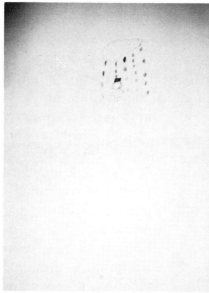

Figure 17   *A self-portrait drawn unusually small.*

30

body parts. When traumatized, a person may regress to an earlier drawing phase or begin to use only a tiny portion of the paper. This regression is often evident immediately following the abuse. If the abuse was repetitive the art work may become arrested at the stage when the abuse began. If someone is functioning at a lower developmental level and appears stuck in this phase, the therapist should assist in helping her to work toward higher functioning. Any intervention needs to be carried through with the least restrictive approach in mind. Trauma severely interferes with trust. Therefore, it is important to remember that the art experience needs to be safe and enjoyable. For example, never draw on someone else's drawing. This is intrusive and violating. I will never forget a college professor who had the habit of marking on MY art work. He thought he was being helpful. I thought he was being obnoxious. (Obnoxious is an adult word used in place of a more colorful word I used then.) If working next to someone who repeatedly draws lines in a fashioned order, the therapist may want to draw circles, squares, and other shapes, on a separate piece of paper. This encourages expanding art expressions by introducing new symbols. Whether the deficit in development is due to deprivation, inaccessibility to art, or the experience of trauma, the results of working within safe, comfortable distances side-by-side can facilitate further development in drawings. It also provides the opportunity to pictorially express trauma.

Sometimes development is made even slower by the tendency to be repetitious and rigid. The tendency is to repeat the familiar and avoid the unfamiliar (sound familiar?) (Figure 18). This behavioral response reflects what any traumatized person does in that the effects of trauma cause the unfamiliar to feel extremely risky. To risk any change, even though it may be healthier, is initially too frightening. Repetition and rigidity become exaggerated due to this fear.

31

For the person who is developmentally disabled this characteristic of familiar repetition appears to originally be associated with pleasure and contentment. They have little interest in the unfamiliar. As a result of this, their art work may reflect obsessive qualities such as continuously repeating a pattern of lines or shapes. This repetitive drawing approach appears to reduce tension and is pleasurable.

Laurie Wilson, an art therapist, states that the person who is developmentally disabled draws in this repetitious manner due to having

Figure 18   *Repetitive art work.*

lived through a prolonged infancy. They are apt to be isolated because of their sensory, perceptual, and intellectual deficits. Their emotional immaturity causes them to be even more isolated (Wilson, 1977). What I have observed is when traumatized, the need to perform repetitiously is further perpetuated, especially if the abuser was a caregiver or someone they were dependent on during infancy. Wilson states that isolation inevitably diminishes their opportunities for normal object relations that would otherwise stimulate the development of sensory, perceptual, and cognitive capacities. This causes self-stimulating behaviors, placidity, or both. The final result is repetitiousness and inflexibility. As stated earlier, this type of behavior often is evident when traumatized. Increased inflexibility and repetitiousness occur because the sense of trust has been violated. This makes change extremely frightening and development of normal relations difficult.

Repeated patterns in art work and in behavior could have some of its roots in early self-stimulating behavior that occurs with the infant who is developmentally disabled. When traumatized, at any age, this type of behavior can be reactivated or reinforced. Therefore, people with disabilities who have been abused will have even more difficulty moving beyond this early stage. To be transfixed in this stage of development does not promote healing or growth. Without intervention it may feel like being caught in a revolving door with no obvious escape.

It is important for the therapist to help facilitate clients to find the exit in the revolving door and move toward growth. They can be persuaded to slowly take small steps and work toward a more complex level of functioning. The therapist can introduce safe opportunities through art medium. The therapist needs to work side by side using hand-over-hand techniques and mirror healthy boundaries while teaching control and building trust. An example of moving to a more complex level through art can occur when introducing paint for the first time. It may progress from water and sand to paint. This proceeds as follows: 1. Begin by introducing water and sand to experience pleasurable tactile stimuli. Encourage touching and playing with the sand and water. 2. When comfortable with this, water can be tinted. Encourage drawing with the tinted water and finger on paper. 3. Gradually, colored sand is introduced. Mixing and drawing with fingers in the colored sand can then be demonstrated. Eventually, include the use of paint brushes. 4. Finally, more complex stimuli are introduced, such as paint with large brushes. This process may take a long period of time but will help the client move beyond repetition and promote growth.

3

A Picture IS Worth a Thousand Words

Illustrative Examples

It never ceases to amaze me how powerful and healing creating art can be. Survivors of trauma for the first time may express their feelings. For the first time they may begin to feel in control. And for the first time they may experience some relief from the secret they have carried for so long. Through creativity they are able to go deeply into difficult emotions. Alice Miller in her book, *The Untouched Key: Tracing Childhood Trauma in Creativity and Destructiveness,* suggests that artists are intuitively compelled to find expression for what they were forbidden to speak as a child (Miller, 1990). I find this true not only for artists but for all who have been affected by trauma. Art is a safe way to communicate what one has experienced or is experiencing. For the person whose vocabulary and speech process are limited, it is important to provide a safe environment and alternative ways to express themselves.

To illustrate the power and healing potential of art I am including a few case examples from art therapy sessions. These were chosen to illustrate how art can be implemented in a variety of therapeutic ways. Art can be used by a person with a disability as an aid to help illustrate images such as those from nightmares, to emphasize or better understand a feeling, and to discharge traumatic images. Each example represents the potential of art as an alternative to traditional verbal communication. There are times when art work is created in sessions and I am deeply affected. The passion and fervor that is poured into some pieces have a powerful impact on me. These pieces are examples of extremely passionate and powerful expressions of art.

Rick, an adolescent, had been in counseling for approximately one half year. He had used the art materials on only a few occasions. When he did it was usually with three dimensional medium such as wood or clay. Rick has a developmental disability and his speech is difficult to comprehend. He was in many ways a teenager with typical adolescent concerns, except when it came to his biological family. His was not the ideal family.

He was removed from his family due to severe abuse of all kinds. He was placed with relatives. They genuinely cared for him but he became difficult to control. He was then moved to a group home serving people with disabilities who have behavioral problems. His history of physical, emotional, and sexual abuse was horrendous.

Rick's immediate family renewed their interest in him every six months to a year. The reason for this was unclear but it did occur just around tax season. Their interest meant the possibility of court involvement. Rick was extremely frightened by this process. In the past his family repeatedly had police contact while Rick resided with them. Rick was terrified of the possibility of having to return to his biological family.

When Rick's mother again expressed her "interest" in regaining custody of him, the staff at the group home became concerned. Rick appeared depressed, aggressive behaviors increased, and he expressed confusion about his future. Just prior to a meeting with his caseworker about this situation, Rick came in for a counseling session. I immediately noticed the change in Rick. He was withdrawn and made no eye contact. I asked him a number of questions regarding adolescent concerns and interests. I tried everything from girls to music. He did not respond orally to any of my questions. I decided to use art to try to facilitate a conversation and to help us both understand what he was feeling.

I sat down next to him with paper and markers. I explained to him that I was going to draw some pictures and if he wanted to he could add to the drawing. To engage his interest I began by drawing a simple picture of him. While drawing, I asked him questions as to what details he wanted me to include. He pointed to the "tail" in his hair which I then added. I continued to ask questions. I pointed out that something seemed to be bothering him. No answer. I offered suggestions. When I mentioned family he sat up and nodded his head yes. I questioned further for specifics. He answered "yes" to mother. I asked him if I could draw a picture of her. He shook his head "yes". While drawing his mother, he spontaneously told me that she was shorter than he was and had longer hair. I kept the drawing very simple and added these details.

I asked him if he wanted to add anything to the picture. Eventually, he picked up a green marker and colored in his mother's hair. Next he took red and with a quick, deliberate stroke he circled her mouth. He gradually became more attentive and made eye contact with me as he continued to work on the drawing with a black marker. He obliterated the hands and feet of his mother. He paused and looked at this for a moment. He then scratched out the eyes and the body with bold, angry marks. Finally, he added a black line, separating himself from his mother. He sat back and viewed what he had just accomplished. I

Figure 19   *Rick's drawing* .

37

asked him if there was anything else he wanted to add. He picked up a brown marker and drew a bat in his hand. He slumped back into the couch. He was visibly upset and depleted upon completion of the drawing. I talked to him about his feelings, how he had a right to these. He quietly listened (Figure 19).

I put out another piece of paper. I drew different facial expressions. He drew faces indicating sad and tired feelings. At the end of this session Rick no longer avoided eye contact with me and had become increasingly verbal. He appeared relieved. The art work was a vehicle for him to express the forbidden: his rage toward his mother. This rage was related not only to the current custody issue but to a lifetime of confusion, hurt, and fear. Following this session, Rick began to express some of these feelings to staff and clearly let his caseworker know how he felt. Custody was never granted back to the biological family. Although Rick does not use art as his primary means of communicating, on this occasion when the words were too difficult to speak he found a safe avenue to discharge disturbing emotions that were interfering with daily functioning.

During an art therapy group I had the privilege of meeting Dana. She was a young woman in her mid-twenties with developmental disabilities. Dana was extremely verbal, energetic, and sensitive. She talked openly about the sexual abuse that she had experienced in the past. In fact, one of the reasons for her referral to the group was that she perseverated on the topic to the point that it interfered with daily activities.

The art therapy group involved seven members with developmental disabilities, all of whom had experienced sexual trauma. Dana was the first to talk about her sexual abuse. For many members this was their first group experience. They initially were uncomfortable talking so openly about the abuse.

Not Dana! To help the group function cohesively it was important to gradually bring the topic of sexual abuse into the group. Trust needed to be established before such open discussions would be tolerated by all the members. Therefore, I had to assist Dana with boundaries yet provide a place for her to discharge these feelings. I encouraged the group to talk about their comfort levels on various topics. The group began to realize that everyone had different boundaries. We discussed what alternatives there might be if some people had a difficult time listening to certain topics. This discussion encouraged Dana to find other outlets for her sexual abuse issues. She developed awareness that boundaries are essential because talking about some things to the wrong people may only prove to be retraumatizing.

Art became the vehicle for Dana to express her feelings about the sexual abuse. She especially enjoyed using clay because of the three dimensional qualities. It was as if she needed this extra dimension to express the reality of her experiences. In one session she asked to sculpt a figure of herself. With my assistance she began to build the figure. During the process she talked about the places she was physically and sexually hurt. She pointed to the vaginal area of the sculpture saying, "Bad things there". I helped her to understand that the vagina is not bad, that what happened to her was bad. She seemed to understand this difference and even appeared somewhat relieved. She then carefully sculpted this area. She repeated this procedure with the breasts and buttocks. Each time she carefully molded the area and stroked it as if to say, "It's okay now." When completed she said, "This is me, I like me, Dana not bad."

After the clay figure was fired she wanted to paint it. This was two weeks later. This time she did not feel so good about the piece. She led a group discussion about private parts, and demanded that the sculpted parts be kept covered stating they were bad. The group, now more comfortable with this topic, responded similarly. I educated the group on privacy, the positives about the body and what to do when the body is violated. Following this discussion the group painted their clay pieces. Dana continued to look at her piece with discomfort. I asked her what was wrong. She replied that her figure needed to be covered. I offered a tissue and suggested that she paint clothes on it. She eventually took red paint and aggressively covered the body with it. When I talked to her about this she said, "Bad, bad". She was not grasping the prior conversation as she had when sculpting this piece. I sensed there was more to this for her.

I spent some time with her individually and talked about these feelings. She described to me an incident that occurred in the group home that morning, where she was reprimanded for soiled clothing. This evidently reminded her of past abuse. She talked to me about the shame and guilt she experienced as a result of her past sexual abuse. I helped her to separate the bad things that were done to her body from the good things about her body by referring to the clay figure. Following this conversation she again began to caress her clay figure and carefully put it in a safe place. (Figure 20)

Figure 20 *Dana's clay sculpture.*

Dana also constructed a tile collage made from clay. This piece was one of the last ones that she created in the group. It represented four facets in her life: a personal interest, a feeling, the abuse, and a safe place to live. Dana began to learn how to set limits and boundaries. She began to focus on other important aspects in her life. For the time being her life was not just made up of the abuse. In group she shared more with them than just the

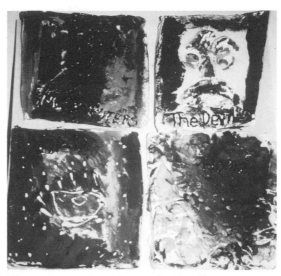

Figure 21   *Dana's ceramic tile collage.*

sexual trauma alone. She found alternatives to expressing her emotions about the abuse. Art became a safe, visually validating, and highly expressive avenue for Dana to cope with the reality of her painful trauma. (Figure 21) She also found positive qualities about herself that helped her to build self-confidence and self-esteem.

Nightmares are frequently illustrated in art work, especially in pieces done by famous artists. These images are often terrifying and violent. Words are never enough to describe the essence of a nightmare experience. Have you ever tried explaining a nightmare? Through art there is an opportunity to visually describe what occurs in the nightmare. The art can help to understand and make sense of a horrifying nighttime event. The nightmare may even be recurring, which intensifies the experience. Repetitive nightmares can be so overwhelming that even in the waking state they cannot be forgotten. This was the case for Bobby, an eleven year-old with a developmental disability. He was referred to art

41

therapy due to emotional and behavioral problems that were interfering in the school classroom. One of the underlying stressors causing these problems was a recurring nightmare he had been having.

For the first couple of sessions Bobby drew a series of pictures. They were of burning houses. He began with a pencil drawing of the house. He would then always insist on using paint. The piece ultimately ended covered in black paint. He appeared frightened and anxious as he aggressively attacked the paper (Figure 22). I

thought that maybe the paint was not an appropriate medium at the time. But something told me that he needed to master the paint. So I did not intervene. Gradually he began to control the paint by covering only a portion of the original drawing. He started

Figure 22   A recurring nightmare.

to talk more openly about the nightmare, in vivid details. These details had never been discussed up to this point. Color began to appear in the paintings.

In the final painting of this series, Bobby carefully chose different colors and clearly illustrated his nightmare in a much more realistic approach. When this piece was completed Bobby stated, "This is it, this is what I see when I close my eyes" (Figure 23). He did not appear anxious or frightened about this nightmare anymore. He was quite proud of this accomplishment. This was the last time that he drew or painted this nightmare. He had mastered the demon and could now move on. Bobby's behavior began to improve in school and he was able to concentrate for longer periods of time. Whether these nightmares stemmed from a real event, or were

Figure 23   *The nightmare is mastered.*

connected with unconscious feelings associated with home, was not the issue or concern for this series. Bobby needed to feel in control of the nightmare so that it no longer controlled him. Later, the goal was to understand the root of these nightmares, but for the time this clearly met Bobby's needs. The art provided a safe place to illustrate the images that were so terrifying to Bobby. Each drawing and painting was a step toward mastering, organizing and expressing this experience.

4
The Journey

It is important to understand the entire therapeutic process that occurs in an art therapy session. Often I am asked to assess a drawing that I was not present for during the art making process. What many people fail to understand is that the road to getting there is as important as the final destination. There is so much that occurs throughout the journey. It can only be understood if one went along for the ride. The end result may be a dusty vehicle, an empty tank of gas, or a new bump or scratch on the door. What about the events that led to those apparent results? Only the driver and the passenger really know what happened, unless the passenger was asleep.

The therapist must participate in the journey. She needs a thorough knowledge of the elements that affect the art making experience. This includes familiarity with the physical properties of the art medium and the complexity of each task at every level of the creative process. For example, watery paint that is difficult to control may result in frustration and rapidly evoke regression in the person's behavior and art work (Figure 24). A drawing may begin with rendered detail

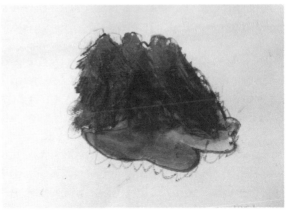

Figure 24   *Underneath is a carefully rendered drawing.*

but if paint is used to add color the result may be a blurred mess. Paint inherently evokes regression due to the nature of the medium. It can not be controlled in the same way a pencil or marker can be controlled. The therapist needs to be aware of this and be ready to offer other materials that would compliment the original drawing.

The art therapist observes details, an alert passenger on the journey of art making. The journey begins when the person enters the room and ends when they exit. Everything that occurs throughout the course of the session is significant. It is important to be aware of nonverbal behaviors such as where the person chooses to sit or what material she decides to work with, as well as what influenced these decisions. These details provide essential information for the art therapist about the person's present and past situation. For example, a person may attempt to possess or dominate the art materials. This may be indicative of a need for control or desire for attention. These behaviors could stem from neglect, abuse, or deprivation. Another important detail is being aware of erasures. These may indicate confusion, ambivalence, or frustration in relation to either past or present events. Erasures or mistakes are often significant, as these tend to be connected with the unconscious.

Art therapist Judith Rubin points out that when art is used for therapy or evaluation it is not a simplistic tool and does require serious training. She states, "Art is a powerful tool, one which, like a surgeon's must be used with care and skill if it is to penetrate safely beneath the surface." A seemingly simple art task can elicit powerful feelings and sensations that can be harmful (Rubin, 1984). For example, what appears to be a routine request for a drawing about Christmas may trigger terrifying memories for a person who was abused during the holidays. (Figure 25) A self-portrait may appear to be a natural task, however if sexual abuse has occurred, the person may re-experience the trauma to their body when drawing a picture of themselves. A self-portrait is often met with resistance, anger, rage, regression, or withdrawal if the abuse involved violation of the body. Self drawings are not

Figure 25   *An idealized image of Christmas.*

only difficult for those who have been traumatized but for any person who suffers from even the slightest low self-esteem. Think about it. How would you react if someone asked you to draw a picture of yourself? This type of drawing is commonly suggested by therapists. If art is to be used in therapy we need to be cautious about what we ask our clients to draw.

Appropriate art supplies, such as different sizes of paper and a variety of materials, are needed to allow for choice and control. When working with traumatized individuals many issues will surface that are associated with lack of control. Allowing them to make choices and providing opportunities to feel some control can safely occur in art therapy sessions. At times it can be helpful to devise projects with the client that are carefully planned. These planned projects offer many choices and when completed allow for a sense of accomplishment. Having high quality materials available to choose from gives the message that the client is important and deserving of making art with good supplies. It is a pleasure to watch those who have had limited choices walk into art therapy sessions with an array of materials available. Eyes widen and smiles emerge. They feel respected and privileged. This will result in a successful and positive experience that will build confidence, rather than add to everyday frustrations and negativism.

It is important to encourage the artist to interpret their own art work, if ANY interpretation is done at all. I am reminded of the well-meaning teacher or parent whose child proudly comes to them with a picture she had just labored over. The adult's response to this may be, "Oh, what a beautiful house." The child instantly retracts the picture and timidly (or angrily) responds, "It is not a house. It is a picture of me." The child feels diminished and the adult may feel quite foolish. This common scenario illustrates that disclosure of the contents in the art work should come from the artist, and only when the artist is ready. Open ended, nonjudgemental questions are safe to ask. Direct interpretative ones are not.

The most damaging result of trauma is the loss of trust. This loss of trust requires long-term therapeutic interventions to assist in rebuilding it. Once the person begins to feel safe enough to express themselves through art it may then take additional time to establish enough trust to talk about their art work. No matter what the content is, the art therapist validates and supports all art expressions. This demonstrates the therapist's willingness to accept them for who they are and what they feel. In return this helps to build the trust that is necessary for self-disclosure.

I am an advocate for encouraging the use of creative expression in therapy, even if the therapist is not an art therapist. Creative expression should be part of therapeutic work when healing from sexual abuse or any other trauma. Due to managed care and the current climate of the mental health profession, it is important that therapists who work with people with developmental disabilities become educated in alternative therapy modalities. However, it is important to be aware of the power that art has when utilized in therapy. Interpretation and in-depth use of art therapeutically does require extensive training and background in art therapy, as well as the knowledge of the application of art materials. A referral to an art therapist is recommended when art becomes a primary focus, or when more in-depth work is needed involving the creative process.

5

Visual Reality

As far as I am aware, there has been very little research on the art work of those with disabilities who have been traumatized. The material provided here has been from my experience working with this population. Art therapy is an important part of the healing process for this population and sometimes the only way to heal from trauma due to limited range of communication. Unfortunately, there continues to be those with primitive beliefs that these issues are better left alone.

A staff person in a residential setting expressed his personal feelings about counseling. He stated that an intense psychiatric medication approach and a "male role model" would be more than sufficient. Art therapy was not needed for the client with limited expressive and receptive communication skills. This statement followed a very serious incident in which the client had sexually assaulted a staff person. The incident appeared to have been related to recurrent flashbacks. The flashbacks often caused him to behave in the same way as his perpetrator had behaved. The statement by the staff person, that it was better to medicate and distract this client rather than treat the core of the problem, quite frankly "pissed me off". After I calmed down, I informed him as to how I felt, although I used more professional language in the description of my feelings. I do not and will not hide my rather strong opinions about such issues. People with developmental disabilities have been neglected in the mental health field and I cannot remain silent. That certainly will not be effective if change in our society is to ever occur.

Art provides a powerful way to succinctly and effectively express complex feelings that otherwise may fester internally and become destructive. In Miller's book she writes, "Disassociated from the original cause, their feelings of anger, helplessness, despair, longing, anxiety, and pain will find expression in destructive acts against others or against themselves" (Miller, 1990). What better way to discharge these feelings than through a safe, nonverbal visual approach? In this section I have identified specific themes that are commonly expressed in the art work of those people with developmental disabilities who have been traumatized. These include: anxiety and fear; aggression and anger; depression; denial; lack of self-esteem; and regression.

Fear and Anxiety

In general, anxiety and fear may be displayed through regressed, kinestheticly formed art expressions. People with developmental disabilities tend to draw in a more primitive style, but when traumatized their art can appear even more regressed. The art materials may be used to play or mess with, resulting in images that are blurred or covered over. Anxieties and fears may be expressed as animals, or dark, concealed im-

Figure 26   *Garfield in an unnatural state.*

ages (Figure 26). These images may be a personal perception of an abuser and the feelings are expressed through drawings of animals that are frightening or threatening.

52

When traumatized it can be healing to draw the experience, and by doing so it offers a measure of cathartic relief and an opportunity to develop a sense of control over a situation where there was no control. People with disabilities are not commonly encouraged to vent their fears or emotions. Their fears may even be viewed as distorted or insignificant. No matter who the person is, fears are never insignificant. They can be distorted but it still does not mean it is not real for them. Externalizing and discharging fears within a selective safe place reduces perseveration on the trauma. Perseveration may occur when one is unable to release the feelings associated with trauma. The therapeutic environment can become a safe container to gain some mastery over the event and experience a sense of control. Art can significantly reduce fears and anxieties.

The therapist needs to assess when the time is appropriate for assisting the client in releasing repressed and dissociated emotions resulting from their trauma. However, a person who is flooded by memories or is overwhelmed with anxiety needs to first establish some control in relation to these feelings. Therefore, I often recommend that the client draw images that are soothing, calming, or reassuring during times of crises. Staying in the here-and-now is essential when invaded by trauma memories. Any type of art work that may trigger further regression should be avoided. Materials such as crayons, clay or paint that are inherently regressive may not be appropriate at certain times. The art therapist is trained to observe behaviors that may be triggered by the art materials. It is important to be aware of the person's present emotional state when deciding which materials to use. This can help facilitate expression through the materials in the most beneficial and appropriate manner.

Anger and Aggression

Pretty pictures with hearts and flowers may not be what they appear. This may be a defense. Art work that appears highly defended may have been created by an internal need to maintain control over feelings of aggression and anger. When traumatically violated these

Figure 27   *Red and black dominate this drawing.*

feelings are highly charged and often difficult to express. The disabled have been taught "not to make a scene", to behave themselves or to remain quiet. These messages are the foundation for building up highly concentrated defenses. This interferes with the natural human need to express strong feelings.

Expression of anger or aggression in drawings may be displayed through infantile scribbling or through the use of heavy, thick, and jagged lines. Common colors used to express these feelings are red and black (Figure 27). Drawings may contain aggressive looking images as monsters or people who appear frightening or are distorted.

Depression

Depression and shame can certainly diminish the urge to be creative, or result in complete withdrawal. We have all probably experienced a diminished urge to do something at one time or another. Abuse can cause people to feel unworthy and unloved, and experience low self-esteem that can lead to depression. Research indicates that there is a high rate of depression among people with developmental disabilities (Courtois, 1988). Creating art can open a window to what is going on internally. It allows one to visually explore the root of the depression. This visual opportunity can help decrease feelings of depression and the desire to withdrawal.

Images that are drawn significantly smaller, with little or no motion, clinging to edge of the paper for security or darker than usual may be an indication that depression is prevalent (Figure 28). Since motivation to create is often de-

Figure 28   *This house drawing reflects depression.*

pleted when depressed, it is important to offer incentives to increase the desire to produce art. This may require that the therapist provide an enticing environment that encourages creative expression. I have been known to do some "eccentric" (I prefer playful) things with the art materials to demonstrate their diverse and wonderful potential. By turning on upbeat music and arranging a variety of materials with which to express oneself, it is hard not to join in the fun! I will often playfully create art along side of someone who is hesitant. With the gentle persuasion of seeing someone else enjoy creating art, and by providing a safe environment to do so, it is difficult to resist. Collage is another way to increase motivation. By having an array of pre-cut magazine pictures available and demonstrating the possibilities with this medium, art making is often facilitated. (Figure 29).

Denial

Inevitably, denial is encountered at some point in the recovery process from trauma. Denial originates very early from predominant messages that talking about the abuse is prohibited. Denying the abuse made it easier to cope with at the time. The victim of the abuse may also feel that the abuse was their fault or per-

Figure 29   *A magazine picture inspired this artist to embellish it with his creative drawings.*

ceive the abuse as normal behavior. Information about abuse and also what does not constitute abuse may be required to help break through any denial. Perpetrators not only take advantage of their victims sexually, but also emotionally. With people who have a developmental disability, they also take advantage of their cognitive limitations.

In art work, this denial may take on the guise of fences, walls, and other encased objects, or emerge as stereo-types of flowers or rainbows (Figure 30). Moving beyond denial is essential, as it will become a stumbling block in recovery. Art work can help to work through denial. For instance, when a wall is drawn in a picture, I will encourage looking beyond the wall to imagine what is behind it, or what is holding it up. For those with limited communication skills I may work in a more concrete

Figure 30   *A "pretty" rainbow.*

manner. One way of doing this is to actually build walls together in three dimensional forms using cardboard or clay. I encourage clients to break down the walls, figuratively. It is loud, but effective. My colleague just loves this and it is especially interesting depending on who is in her office at the time of the therapeutic "break though." Luckily, she is used to my unconventional means and approves of them.

Lack of Self-Esteem

People with disabilities are taught to obey caregivers and those in authority, under all types of conditions. Often they have no other alternative but to obey as a result of physical or mental limitations. This compliance creates situations in which those who live within systems are easily manipulated and abused. In return they often blame themselves for the abuse, or perceive themselves as bad because of the abuse. The disabled are constantly reminded of their disabilities in negative ways. Other people decide for them what behaviors need improvement. These controlling people seldom take into account that the disability may make the so called improvement impossible. Those at the blunt end of this kind of service end up feeling like they have failed. This further decreases self-esteem.

Art work reflecting poor self-image may appear self-deprecating or contain negative statements and feelings. Drawings that reflect low self-esteem may contain light, vague, or broken lines. Feelings of powerlessness are often illustrated by using only small portions of the paper (refer to Figure 28). Images may cling to the side of the paper as a young child clings to the mother for safety and reassurance.

People with disabilities are often physically intruded upon by their caregivers, or other people involved in daily care. They may feel that their bodies do not belong to them. When abused, this feeling intensifies and further difficulties associated with body boundaries are common. Distorted images of the human body may be illustrated in art work. Sexual imagery may be drawn large or appear confused. Body parts may not be connected, or may be omitted completely in the drawings. With those who have developmental disabilities this seems to appear in art work even without the occurrence of trauma. I have found this to be associated with the feeling of being out of control of one's body as a result of dependence on others for their bodily care.

Regression

Regression with art materials that are difficult to control, such as paint or clay, is common. Have you ever played in the mud? When was the last time you did this? For some it was yesterday, for others not since childhood. What images come to your mind? If you never played in the mud due to some compulsive cleanliness thing then this may be difficult. Imagine yourself playing in wet, soft, pliable mud. What comes to mind? It may stimulate some feelings related to childhood or the last time you changed an infant's diaper. Some art materials can trigger similar regressive responses because of the nature of working with fluid substances. Moving toward earlier forms of expression can be healthy, as it can have a relaxing and calming effect. Nevertheless, these materials can also prematurely release disturbing and highly emotional content which may be overwhelming (Figure 31).

Figure 31   *Disturbing context is released.*

As discussed earlier, it is important to be aware of the artistic developmental level in which the person works. Sometimes what looks to be regression in art expressions may be more accurately be related to the person's developmental level. It is also important to know the person's artistic style prior to when the abuse occurred. Trauma will effect artistic expression and appear in the form of regression. Art work done immediately following a trauma commonly contains smearing, tearing, perseveration, or infantile scribbling. These approaches may be pleasurable, safe, and reassuring while they counteract the anxiety and fear of the trauma that occurred. If, however, these perseverative and regressive responses continue for an extended period of time, it will interfere with potential creative and emotional growth.

6

The Art of the Matter

In *Breaking the Silence*, author Cathy Malchiodi addresses and describes common graphic indicators in art productions of children who have been sexually abused. She states, "How the trauma of sexual abuse is expressed visually in the art production cannot be generalized easily or concisely" (Malchiodi, 1990). This is important for all clinicians to be aware of as too often art work is misinterpreted. There are many variables that need to be accounted for before art can be analyzed. It is important to be cognizant of these variables with children who have been sexually abused. It is equally important to be aware of these factors with people who are developmentally disabled and have been traumatized. Factors emphasized by Malchiodi include: knowing how the person may react to certain situations, when the abuse occurred, the extent of the abuse, the age of the victim, and the phase of the crisis when the drawing occurs. She states that these and additional issues will be reflected in the drawings. With those who are developmentally disabled these factors are also apparent in their art work. For example, a specific color or texture may trigger an aberrant reaction in the art work. Red may evoke anger, as it may be a reminder of a particular bloody incident. It could be abuse related or it may be due to a pre-trauma incident, and therefore not be related to recent trauma. This information is essential, as it could be easily misinterpreted.

I have observed these indicators of sexual abuse that Malchiodi identifies in the art work of those who have a developmental disability. These similarities, as well as additional characteristics, will briefly be discussed. Examples from drawings that I collected in various art therapy sessions with folks with disabilities will illustrate the common graphic art indicators of abuse.

Distorted Bodies

Body imagery may appear deformed in trauma-based art work. When traumatized the human figure drawing can elicit feelings of anger, fear, shame, and ambivalence. These emotions will effect how the human figure is drawn. The effects of long-term trauma can alter thought processes and interfere with visual expression, with regard to both content and style. Drawings of bodies may appear disorganized as the result of feelings

Figure 32   *Body parts may be lacking.*

associated with the trauma. The body may be lacking entirely or drawn without the lower half (Figure 32). Parts of the body may be exaggerated, especially any area associated with the abuse. The lower half may be neglected in the drawing, possibly indicating denial or fear. Unconsciously this expresses repressed emotions about the abuse.

Color

The store where I purchase my art materials must wonder what I do. Many times I just buy red and black Craypas or pastels. I can hear them now, whispering to each other as I leave, "She must be a very angry person." The people that I work with are angry and rightly so. Red and black are used most often, and with the most vigor and intensity. When these colors dominate the art work it may be an indicator of some type of trauma (Figure 33). Other colors that may be repeatedly used with people who are developmentally disabled are yellow and brown. These are often associated with areas of the body that have been violated or damaged when traumatized. The use of color of those who have a developmental disability will depend on their developmental level, so it is important not to assume their color choice is deliberate. It may be

Figure 33   *Red and black stripes are dominant.*

connected with preference or convenience, the closest color within reach. Our first instinct may be to think the worst if we come across a drawing of a person colored entirely red. However, you may find that red is associated with warmth and comfort.

Enclosure

As a teenager, I lived in another country with my family for a few years. One of the first things that I noticed there was that almost every house had large brick walls around its perimeters. I did not understand why at first. Fences are usually used for either keeping something in, or keeping something out. In my old neighborhood, the only houses with fences around them were those neighbors who were either unfriendly or owned vicious dogs. So did that mean everyone was unfriendly in this new country, or that they all had vicious dogs? One day, I sat on top of the wall. I had nothing better to do, so I finally figured it out.

The walls were needed to keep the gigantic, Jurassic sized rats out of the yards! The fences were needed for protection.

Figure 34   *A clay padlock is added.*

Art work that contains walls, fences, or heavy lines that enclose other figures may be an expression of the desire for protection. (I both understood and desired this protection once I realized what was on the other side of the wall.) Feelings of being unsafe and unprotected are common among those who have been traumatized. For example, a young man in an art therapy session sculpted a self-portrait from clay. When he completed this he stated that he was very uncomfortable with this piece. He said, "It needs something." Without any hesitation he made a large padlock out of clay. He said, "No one can get to him unless they are given the key" (Figure 34). It was clear that he wanted no one to have access to the key unless he chose who was safe enough to have it. He needed to feel protected. Imagery can provide this safeguard. I often encourage the client to imagine a safe place. The images that are commonly drawn are: a room filled with comforting items; a bubble that no one can pop; a see-through container with no entrance; a protective shield; and a field with flowers and high grass in which to hide. All these images are protective and enclosed. Having experienced abuse took away the feeling of safety. It can feel safe, even if only temporary, to create these situations in imagery.

Disconnected Imagery

Art work may appear highly disorganized. Images may be drawn all over the paper with seemingly no purpose. It may resemble the art work that one does while speaking on the phone. In this case it is usually an unconscious attempt at organizing our thoughts or trying to keep busy while talking to a boring or annoying person. For those who have been traumatized it may be an attempt to organize internal chaos that is created by the abuse. The artist may not feel grounded because of overwhelming emotions connected with trauma. Images are scattered or float across the paper. Drawing can be an attempt to depict a specific event or emotion, however, in doing so one becomes flooded with physical, emotional, or sexual flashbacks. As a learned response for survival, trauma victims disconnect from themselves when sensorily overloaded. Trauma survivors will often speak of the abuse experience as one of feeling distant from the actual event (Figure 35). This description is the process called dissociation. It will appear in art work as floating, distorted or disconnected imagery.

Figure 35   *Illustration of "dissociation".*

65

7

A Palette of Possibilities

My art therapy sessions are rarely planned. They occur spontaneously depending on individual needs. I use many different techniques that encourage creative responses. Not all these techniques are something you may want to try. Many require that you become familiar with the materials before attempting to use them. If art is to be used in therapy sessions it is important that you do have basic supplies on hand. Chart 2 outlines art materials recommended to have available in the office. If you are adventurous and plan to use the "messier" materials be sure to have plenty of cleanup supplies available. If you do not have a sink nearby baby wipes work wonders. Paper towels and water in a large container are needed if paint is to be used.

I find myself continuously creating new techniques when others are not appropriate for a particular person. This assures that the person will have the opportunity to fully express themselves in a creative, fresh and successful manner. They are offered a palette full of endless possibilities. I will briefly outline a few of the techniques that I have implemented in my art therapy sessions.

Puppet Projects

Puppets can be made out of a variety of materials and in so many diverse ways. The nature of puppet making allows for self-expression through two different means. To begin with, there is the process of constructing them. The actual construction of the puppet requires decision making, problem solving, creativity, and so much more. Secondly, is using the puppet for role playing.

Chart 2

Recommended Art Materials

Restrictive Materials	**Name Brand**
Colored Pencils	Berol Prisma color
Thin and thick markers	Crayola
Crayons	Crayola
Pastels-chalk	Nupastels or Alphacolor
Pastels-oils	Craypas oil pastels
Craypas	-----------------------

Fluid Materials (These are the messier ones!)

Water color paint	Prang
Acrylic paint	Liquitex basic acrylic color
Plasticine	--------------------------
Finger paints	Crayola
Clay	Self hardening
Paper	8½ x 11 White heavier stock
Larger paper for bigger drawings	
Finger-paint paper	
Watercolor paper	
Canvas paper	
Colored construction paper	

Other tools:

Various size paint brushes	newspaper
glue sticks	pencil sharpener
scissors	erasures

Conversations with the creations allows for establishing some distance to voice personal feelings freely and safely through an extension of the self. (Figure 36) Puppets or dolls can become a personal reflection of the artist creating

Figure 36 *Dolls made in an art therapy group.* them. In addition, inside each doll or puppet one can be encouraged to place pieces of paper that contain positive messages written about the puppet maker. When needed, these messages can be referred to as a reminder of their positive qualities and become a source of comfort. Puppets can be used over and over in sessions as vehicles to express difficult feelings. Again, this feels safer because everything comes from the puppet. Store bought and hand made puppets can also be used for psychodramas or role playing.

Clay Modeling

Clay promotes manipulation of a material that is changeable. The pliable and soft characteristics of this medium provide interesting reactions, as was

Figure 37 *An "angelic" clay self-portrait.*

69

discussed earlier. References to forbidden interests in body parts and functions are often elicited. The use of clay stimulates repressed feelings and promotes releasing emotions. The tendency with clay is for one to become less rigid, uninhibited, and highly expressive. The result often reflects personal issues (Figure 37). There are different techniques that can be applied with clay. Free form sculptures can be hand built. Tiles that are rolled out of clay can be developed into a "picture". The tile can be drawn or sculpted on the surface. Containers and handmade pottery pieces can lead to discussions of containment and boundaries, especially when trauma memories become over-whelming. Before clay is introduced be sure that you are familiar with the qualities of this medium, and know how to facilitate its use with success.

Mask Making

Have you ever been to a Halloween party? It is amazing how different people act when dressed up as someone else, or when wearing a mask in disguise. Everyone loosens up and lets down their guard. This same reaction can occur when introduced to making masks. It can be approached in a number of different ways. It can begin with a less threatening approach and advance toward a more involved technique that requires trust. I recommend always beginning with the less threatening approach to help establish some trust and rapport with each other. Masks of this kind can

Figure 38   *A plaster mask.*

be made independently from a relief. The releif may be done over clay, cardboard or paper (Figure 38 and 39). Papier-mâché or plaster is applied over the relief to construct a sturdy mask form. The masks can be an expression of self or an emotion. Details, such as hair, decorations, or other additions may reflect parts of their personalities. The masks can lead to dramatization of an emotion or the abuse, allowing release in a safe and distant manner. The artist can experience feelings of power and control when disguised in a mask.

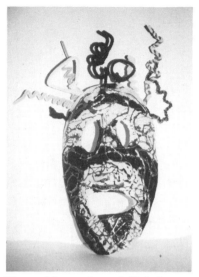

Figure 39 *An embellished plaster mask.*

A more advanced technique that requires well-established trust between the participants is to apply plaster directly over the face. To attempt this type of mask making it is essential to be familiar and comfortable with the properties of plaster. I recommend that you first try this with a well-trusted friend before attempting this with someone who has yet to learn trust. To begin, Vaseline is applied to the face and wet plaster strips are carefully placed on the face to create a relief. This may be a frightening experience since the eyes and mouth are covered for a period of time. Breathing occurs through an opening left under the nose. For those that are able to participate in this type of project, the results will further build trust and establish a sense of boundaries. This type of mask making involves body imagery work since the mask is a relief of their own face. Body imagery work is often neglected with those who have a disability but is very much needed to help build self-esteem.

Spontaneous Paintings

I do not know about you but whenever I see paint opened and ready to go, I cannot resist. It may be the artist in me, but I think it is also a natural desire. An array of bright rich colors in liquid form is difficult to turn down, especially for the person who has been deprived the opportunity of indulging oneself with paint without the confines of pre-fabricated materials. Painting can be emotionally charged because of its vibrancy and looseness. Spontaneous use of paints

Figure 40   *Acrylic paint on canvas.*

can express and communicate ideas, moods, and reactions to the environment, regardless of the person's capacity for representational imagery (Figure 40). The use of paint in therapy sessions requires the therapist to be aware of the media and potential problems that may arise. It will depend on the person's capabilities of handling this liquid material. Initially, the response may be favorable due to the enticing brilliant colors. If an overwhelming response is evoked it is important to assess from where this stems. It may be that too many colors were introduced at once and that the choice of color needs to be reduced. The paper may wrinkle and higher quality paper or canvas is necessary due to a robust and intense approach. The color of the paints may be overwhelming because they are reminiscent of abuse. In this case, paint would not be recommended until more trauma issues are worked through. People with disabilities tend to respond favorably to paint simply because of the provocative qualities.

They enjoy the freedom that paint offers.

Remember Jason whom I spoke about in the preface? He loved to use paint. This was reflected in his beautiful and often fascinating paintings. He approached this material with such vigor and enthusiasm. Jason's robust approach required that he use canvas. Very large ones were his passion (refer to Figure 1). This reduced the frustration of the paper potentially ripping or wrinkling as he worked intensely on his subjects. Interventions were needed at times because Jason had the tendency to overwork his pieces. The therapist can help to reduce potential problems with the art process. This requires knowing the properties of the art materials and knowing the individual using them.

Collage

At one time or another we have all probably made a collage of some type. The best part about collage is going through the magazines to find the right pictures (or article, or recipe, or picture of that great looking guy or girl). The National Geographic magazine was the best! We would spend most of our time looking at nude people from different countries. We were in awe of the distorted looking body parts (to a pre-adolescent that is what they looked like). No one warned us that one day our bodies would take those shapes. In fact, most of the time was spent on

Figure 41   *Creating a collage.*

73

looking at the pictures in magazines which could be quite distracting. I found this was true in art therapy sessions, so I began to provide precut pictures instead of the whole magazine. I am such a spoilsport! Still, you would be surprised at what 15 year old boys and girls can find, even without the whole magazine to look through.

The use of magazine pictures that are precut is enticing, and an inherently manipulative medium. It allows choices in pictures that are of interest. They can be altered and arranged in any way that fits an idea or theme. It is a concrete operation that lessens resistance, and can decrease inhibition with little opportunity for failure. It encourages the use of the imagination. Simple words and phrases can be available that have been precut from magazines. These can be used alone or with pictures. Collage can be very powerful, especially when embellished with drawings or design (Figure 41).

Spontaneous Drawing and Drawing Directives

These techniques may be the simplest, most readily available and allow for the most creativity. Drawings can produce much information about sensory, intellectual, and developmental capacities from those who would otherwise have

Figure 42   *This drawing illustrates abuse.*

a difficult time disclosing anything about themselves. Spontaneously people will draw what they know, how they feel, imagine, and dream. Drawing provides a situation in which important concepts can be taught. For instance, when a drawing of the abuse is produced the artist will realize that it does not result in their being harmed (Figure 42). Visual expression of

Figure 43   *A drawing directive.*

anger can be a healthy release through a nonverbal, creative approach. One learns that they can express feelings instead of keeping them contained. Drawing is another way of containment, but it allows for expression to occur as well. Drawing directives such as, "Draw a picture of your life and your experiences," (Figure 43) helps to mentally organize, put feelings into perspective, and sort out both positive and negative aspects of one's life. Other drawing directives may include: draw a safe place, create a book about yourself or express a feeling.

Books and Journals

Creating a book, writing in a journal, or reading about trauma are all important components of trauma therapy. Therapists can use these creative means to help encourage body awareness, and to teach appropriate and inappropriate touch. Reading from books that focus on these topics may be helpful. To retain the information read from books, I encourage drawing about the specific concepts that are addressed in the readings. This reinforces what is learned and visually gives something in which to refer. It is important to determine the level of understanding and vocabulary of the child when choosing the books. (See Bibliography)

Journaling, the writing of one's thoughts, feelings, dreams and flashbacks, can be a source of emotional release. The journal can serve as a transitional object between sessions or when the therapist is unavailable due to vacation (yes, vacation!) or illness. The journal can be brought to therapy sessions and referred to as a reminder of what occurred from session to session. Drawings, poems, or writing can help a person who was traumatized to record material that is often confusing. It can serve as a permanent and helpful record for reviewing. Visuals are not subject to lapses in memory.

Another technique is constructing handmade books about their abuse. This can be helpful when someone is struggling with denial, or is trying to make sense of what has happened. The book can help to organize events that have occurred. For instance, when a memory emerges or a feeling arises it can become part of one's book. Self-made books can be available at all times to add to, or to use as a visual reference.

Music

Many people with developmental disabilities are drawn to movement and the rhythm of music. For some, the louder the better! Music expresses the patterns of experience in a less literal, more effective and direct way, through its capacity to reflect emotions. Think about how you react to different music. Our inner life is triggered depending on tones, fluctuations in pace and volume, and lyrics. We tend to learn and store music in our long-term memory. Songs have personal meaning. It is this essential connection between music and emotion that invites the use of music in psychotherapy. Music can be a most effective way to evoke a mood or create a change. It can open a whole new door of communication.

People can preselect specific music to be played for different situations. This music can be used in sessions, or at home. Music can have a calming effect when anxious or upset. Music that uses natural sounds such as water, wind, or the sounds made by dolphins, is especially calming. When someone is having a difficult time expressing a particular feeling, music can be played that may help them get in touch with that feeling.

One person that I work with frequently brings in music to play during sessions. It helps her express certain feelings about particular issues. She feels that these pieces speak to her pain and feelings better than she could ever describe them (although she was pretty good doing it verbally as well). The music helps her focus on issues, and enables her to nonverbally express emotions that she may not otherwise have been able to express. Music can provide a starting point and helps a client remain grounded.

Music can evoke a wide range of feelings so it is important to be aware of the potential impact that certain pieces may have. People will have as many different reactions to music as there are different types of music. Before incorporating the use of music in sessions the therapist needs to inquire about their client's reactions to different types of music. For example, some clients may be overwhelmed or flooded with memories when they hear music that has water sounds in it. This may be due to an attempted or accidental drowning experience. Connections with certain sounds need to be assessed.

Music can be comforting, soothing and nurturing. After a difficult day I certainly can be "de-stressed" by certain music and I use this type of relaxation on a daily basis (the amount of time needed depends on the day!). When a client becomes overwhelmed during a session, soothing music that creates a feeling of safety may be helpful. One technique that I frequently use in art therapy sessions is that of imaging to music. Clients can choose specific music that is comforting. While playing the piece, I encourage them to draw an image that is safe and soothing. This image, whether created with or without music, can be recreated over and over as needed.

Using music in conjunction with creating art can elicit powerful responses. Depending on the type of music (the variety is endless, be creative with it!) it may trigger feelings associated with pain, fear, or pleasurable memories. The clinician's library should contain a variety of music. Classical, New Age, and music written especially for children such as lullabies should not be ignored. Chart 3 outlines suggested music for imaging.

While listening to music, the drawings can provide an additional vehicle to visually express feelings associated with the music. It can potentially tap into unconscious primitive material that may otherwise never be explored, or expressed. Music therapy and dance therapy are also beneficial modalities that help those with developmental disabilities work through trauma issues.

Chart 3

Music for Imaging

Songs for the Inner Child Shaina Noel

Unconditional Love Robin Bordeau

Rain Forest Retreat
Summer Sunsets   Nature's Magic
Gentle Giants of the Sea

Circle 'Round the Moon Michelle Sell

The Romantic Sea of Tranquillity Chris Valentino

The Enchanting Sounds of Dolphin Song Dolphins and Orcas in Concert

Recollections Steve Halpern and Daniel Kobialka

Music for Imaging The Lind Institute

Mozart Piano Concerto 26 Perahia

Tschaikowsky: Symphonic No. 6 "Pathetique" Los Angeles Philharmonic

Reflections Yanni

Vavaldi The Four Seasons Mazel

Favorite classic children's music

(This is an abbreviated list of what is available for music for imaging.)

8

Group Therapy and Creativity

Creative expression coupled with a group situation can be supportive and extremely powerful for assisting in the healing process from trauma. A group experience offers peer support that helps members to process difficult emotions. This can lead to validation of their experiences and feelings. It provides a structured and safe environment that encourages sharing. Support is quickly established because of the initial commonality of life experiences. The visual arts can help to relax defenses and reduce anxiety, leading to a new sense of self understanding.

The goals that are established in creative art therapy groups are similar to those focused on in verbal psychotherapy groups for survivors of trauma (see Chart 4). Sessions are structured to address these issues through the application of creative art techniques. The following description is of an art therapy group. Some of the techniques described can be incorporated into group therapy situations for people who are developmentally disabled and have been traumatized.

The group ideally consists of six members, no younger than eighteen years of age. The groups that I have facilitated have included both men and women. With those who have a disability it is important to be aware of individual communication skills and levels of developmental functioning. The group needs to be functioning at a similar developmental level for optimum success. Prior to the group it would be ideal to assess the clients for appropriateness of group therapy. The members should have had previous therapy that addressed trauma issues. In the group described all members have experienced some form of trauma, specifically sexual abuse. In addition, many have experienced

Chart 4

Goals for Group Therapy

1. Alleviating guilt

2. Decreasing depression, if evident

3. Identifying / expressing anger and other feelings

4. Teaching information about human sexuality

5. Developing assertiveness

6. Building trust

7. Increasing self-esteem and body awareness

8. Improving interpersonal relationship skills

9. Extending communication through visual means

physical and emotional abuse. My groups meet weekly for sixteen sessions with each session lasting an hour and a half. If the group has limited attention capacities then the time may need to be reduced. Depending on the group's interest or opportunity, the group has the option to continue meeting for additional sessions.

Since most members have encountered more than one type of abuse, issues of trust and safety will be pronounced. Like a large over-stuffed suitcase, lack of trust and fear are often brought by the members into the group. The suitcases are heavy obstacles, difficult to move. Packed away are feelings in general and trust in particular. The suitcases need to be lightened. Early sessions focus on establishing trust, safety, protection, and equality. Group sessions tend to naturally divide into three stages: beginning, middle and closure stages. As the group progresses the suitcases can be pushed aside or eventually left at home. The goals listed in Chart 4 are met in various stages that will briefly be reviewed.

Beginning Stage

Mary sat alone, away from the group. She was scared. She trusted no one. Why should she? Everyone significant in her life had hurt her. Her suitcase was particularly heavy.

As stated earlier, the beginning stages of group focus on developing trust, safety, and decreasing fears. Most people will experience this at different degrees when in a group situation. The group will therefore begin with setting up the room so that it is comfortable for all members. We respected Mary's choice of where she sat.

Group discussions tend to focus on space, environment, and

touching. The group is encouraged to form a circle and decide distance and placement. Mary wanted nothing to do with this exercise. Mary made it very clear that her place was against the wall, far from the group. I wondered if Mary would even return to the group.

Seating arrangements may take one or more session, depending on individual issues with trust. It is important to allow the members to choose a comfortable place in the room, as with Mary. This gives them some feeling of control and can decrease their fears and anxiety.

Mary returned to the group. She sat in the same place.

Art materials were introduced. It was a time for pure exploration with the medium. Those who have a developmental disability so often have been deprived of good quality art materials that is important to provide an opportunity where they can discover what the materials can do.

Mary's eyes brightened. She leaned forward. Progress.

The members were encouraged to use the pastels, Craypas, markers, colored pencils, and crayons on 12" by 18" white drawing paper. Demonstration of how to use these materials were needed. The demonstration consisted of using the art materials playfully by drawing simple lines and shapes. Producing a complete picture was not the goal for this session.

Mary watched.

The rest of the group joined in eagerly. The session ended with ample time to reflect feelings associated with the exercise. This occurs at the end of each session. Placing the art work in a central area helps to facilitate discussion. I find that hanging the drawings on a wall while reviewing them can be helpful, as it allows the group to view their art from a different perspective. This provides a structured environment for the group to see all the work together.

To my surprise, Mary showed up for group week after week. To be expected, she sat in the same chair, same place.

The early sessions focused on non-threatening topics. Collage work was introduced to help the members express who they were, what they enjoyed, and what they disliked in a safe way (Figure 44). This encouraged decision making and self-disclosure, and yet did not require actual drawing.

Figure 44   *Warming up with collage.*

Mary leaned forward in her chair. She looked interested.

The collage project allowed group members to learn about each other. They became increasingly comfortable with the art materials.

Mary did not look comfortable, but still looked interested.

Building self-confidence is an important process during the beginning stages of the group. To help facilitate this I pointed out the beauty of each completed collage piece by noting interesting color combinations or themes. Every member beamed. Self-confidence began to build. The suitcases were no longer over-overstuffed, except for Mary's.

In another session, which focused on building safety, the group was encouraged to think about situations where they felt safe.

Mary leaned forward. I could see she was thinking about it.

The members were instructed to form a circle. They were then asked to hold hands and stand close enough to each other to touch shoulders. Some members had difficulty being part of this exercise. I never insist that members do anything in which they are uncomfortable.

Mary took her seat and folded her arms across her chest.

The last part of the exercise was to complete a drawing of a group where they would feel safe.

Mary unfolded her arms. She moved towards the table. I held my breath. Mary picked up a pencil and began to draw.

The session included a discussion around body contact, relationships and safety. The issue of good touch versus bad touch began to surface. At the end of the session the group discussed their drawings.

Mary moved her chair back to the usual place. She folded her arms against her chest. The group ended. Mary left, but her drawing remained on her chair (by mistake?). It was a picture of Mary leaning against the wall in her chair. I think I was supposed to see this drawing. She was telling me that she felt safest here in the group. A few minutes later Mary returned to retrieve her drawing. I handed her the drawing and before I could comment on it she turned to leave. As she walked out the door she hesitated and looked back. Mary smiled.

Part of the beginning stage in group is to further develop trust with peers in order to help promote self disclosure. An activity that focuses on this is to have the group break into threes. One person is placed in the middle of the other two and gently rocked back and forth. Again, some members will have difficulty with this exercise.

Mary did.

This needs to be respected, and with time initially hesitant members may be able to participate in this kind of activity. Processing this exercise as a group focuses on the issues of good touch and bad touch, as well as power and control issues. This then begins to move the group toward disclosing their own sexual abuse experiences.

Middle Stage

During the middle phases of the group, members are encouraged to explore feelings. This can be done through whole body expression to increase body awareness. Psychodramas are one way to provide an opportunity to develop affective vocabulary and expand the ability to express emotions. One exercise is to have each person pick a specific feeling. As a group they discuss this feeling. Following this, members are encouraged to express, through action or movement, this feeling using their whole body.

Mary sat in her chair against the wall. She did not like this exercise.

87

New words may be introduced that additionally describe a general feeling. For instance, the word happy may be introduced. Happiness, like all emotions, can be presented in different shades by use of a variety of words like content, pleased or satisfied, just to name a few. Emotion words, like primary colors can be subtly changed by the mixture of just a bit of another color. While red may be vibrant, a touch of white turns it pink. So too, does happy become content with the addition of just a touch of love. By widening their vocabulary they will be able to better describe their emotions. Expanding communication can be empowering. Verbal discussion of these exercises reflects on the importance of emotions and feelings, how our feelings effect our bodies, and how they can be empowering.

Anger is a significant feeling that is often repressed out of fear, or discouraged by others. In group, during the middle stage, anger is encouraged and redefined as an important and acceptable emotion. It is even stated that it is good to feel angry when anger is appro-

Figure 45   *Masks can represent an emotion.*

priate. In the group, amongst peers, different avenues of expressing anger were explored.

Mary was interested.

Throwing balls at targets, using bats and pillows, pounding clay, drawing anger, and verbalizing anger through role play, can all be used in sessions. Anger masks can be constructed out of large paper bags or with plaster (Figure 45). These can then be used for role playing to further express anger in safe and non-threatening ways. Specific techniques that are used in the group will depend on individual needs.

Mary chose clay.

She was not quiet or calm as she worked with the clay. She could pound that clay like no one else. The group noticed her for the first time. Mary was angry. She loved what she could do with the clay.

Assertiveness is addressed in the middle stages of the group process. Role playing a particular situation that requires assertiveness was introduced. All members were part of the role play and took turns being the assertive, and then the non-assertive person. Both roles proved to be a learning experience.

Mary shouted, "NO!!" the loudest.

Figure 46   *Being assertive in drawings.*

The group was then encouraged to draw the word "NO" (Figure 46). The different way the word was drawn, and its effectiveness were discussed. These evoked feelings directly related to the abuse and the perpetrators. Exploration of abuse issues and self-protective techniques can be safely explored through role play and psychodrama.

89

Closure Stage

This phase occurs around the tenth session and continues until the group terminates. At this point the group was eager to openly discuss their trauma, and how it effected them. This was especially true of Mary's drawings. Drawings of the person or of people who had hurt them were common. The group was encouraged to describe their abusers' characteristics. These were written on a large piece of paper. This helped them to identify potentially dangerous situations and persons. Discussions focused on power and control issues.

Sexual abuse is a severe violation and an intrusion of the body that damages self-esteem. Body imagery work can help members to reestablish positive self-esteem. One technique that I have found to be helpful in this area is focusing on feelings about specific body parts. I gave Mary's group an outline of a body and asked them to fill the body with colors that represent different feelings (Figure 47). When reviewing the drawings, the group pointed out positives about each other as opposed to offering negative comments. The abuse can distort images of the self. These perceptions are internalized. However, what group members perceived about each other was not how they felt about themselves. While individual members felt negative about their own body parts, this view was not shared by others towards them. Group therapy can be conducive to peer discussions about body image. It can lead to removing past distorted images while replacing these images with healthier realistic perceptions.

People who have a developmental disability have a hard time relaxing (don't we all) and are often intensely rigid. In part this may be the result of limited teaching about their bodies and how to pay attention to different physical sensations. It is also connected with having had minimal control over their bodies from childhood. By introducing relaxation techniques it is possible to encourage an in-ternal focus to their physical selves. They are encouraged to visualize their bodies as healing forces. In group I take members through relaxation of various parts of the body. They are asked to visualize parts of their body and connect these with positive images.

Figure 47   *Feelings about body parts.*

Mary closed her eyes as she leaned against the table with the rest of the group. She was relaxing.

Following this kind of activity members were again given the body outline, but this time they were encouraged to choose colors that gave them a sense of power and protection. This led to feelings of improved self-esteem and body image. It can symbolically offer protection and be referred to during times that members were tempted to lug in their suitcase.

Trauma often interferes with the ability to play. Play needs to be reexperienced. This is true not only for those who suffered from trauma, but for many adults. When was the last time you actually gave yourself permission to play? If it was yesterday then good for you. Most of us are too caught up in trying to get everything done from day to day. Through art materials play can be introduced. One topic for a drawing that was given in group was the remembering of a particularly pleasant and fun time. Members were asked to imagine such a time if nothing could be recalled. Finger paints and clay can help naturally facilitate playful feelings. As stated before finger paints and clay can also evoke regressed responses.

Mary was covered in clay. She was having fun.

Music that is exceptionally light and uplifting can be incorporated when the focus is on playfulness. The results with such playful activities are often positive for the members. They begin to recognize the importance of play and what they may have missed as a child.

For final closure, the group was asked to draw what was learned throughout the group experience. During this session they processed their grief and loss of the group experience. They also reflected on the many positives they had encountered in the group. Their drawings illustrated various feelings (Figure 48).

Mary drew a picture of herself at the table with the other members. She was the first to stand up and talk about her drawing. She smiled as she proudly walked out of the room with her drawing. She hesitated at the door. She turned and walked over to me. Mary gave me a hug. I cried.

Figure 48   *Closure.*

Summary

Using psychodrama, relaxation techniques, and creative therapy in a group for people with developmental disabilities helps widen the range of communication. It helps the members to understand and resolve conscious and unconscious problems. The art work provides concrete visuals to refer to time and time again. It provides a record of progress and the areas that continue to need more attention. Role playing helps the members to move toward growth, and provides opportunities to creatively work together toward resolution of the effects of sexual abuse.

As members began to feel more comfortable with the group situation, the change for each individual became clearly evident. Mary was just one example of such change. These changes were observed outside of the group as well, in both residential and work settings. At first many members were withdrawn, isolated and unable to make eye contact. There was difficulty concentrating for long periods of time. By the middle stage of the group most had begun to freely express themselves, participate and share more consistently, and experience a decrease in anxiety. The safety established in the confines of the group, and the opportunity to communicate their pain, was the catalyst for change.

Expressive and creative therapies have been defined by the those with whom I work as a gift. Through the arts, it is often the first time their trauma is validated. It may be the first time they ever shared it. Sometimes it is the first time the trauma is allowed to be spoken out loud! The power of the group, and the creative arts, can provide new ways to communicate that then may lead to becoming a whole person.

9

Conclusion

Expressive therapies help to isolate and organize memories of trauma. Whether expressed through visual arts, music or body work, memories are shared in a more concrete form. This helps those with a developmental disability to grasp the reality of the trauma they have endured. Expressive therapy gives a voice to the unspoken. It transforms what was once destructive into creative growth and healing.

Trauma cannot be easily described in words. If language is impaired it may be virtually impossible to verbalize. This does not mean it never existed. It does. It exists in the past. Its memory haunts today. Abuse and abusive incidents happen more often than people want to admit or believe. The effects of trauma are damaging. Verbal language is not necessary to heal from abuse. Externalizing the pain is needed and is essential, whether done orally or nonverbally. Expressive therapies allow people to communicate their pain. We all have the inherent capacity to creatively express ourselves. (Yes, even you can. I hope I made that point clear.) Sometimes support and interventions may be all that are necessary to facilitate creative expression. All one may need is the opportunity and someone who believes in their potential.

I am constantly amazed by the power of art. It is a beautiful and exhilarating experience when someone recognizes their own potential through art. The group of young children described in the beginning of the book did. Jason did. Mick did. Mary did.

And then there is Jake. He thought he was a failure, a "retard", a disgrace. That was what he was told every day of his life. He never was given even a minute of reprieve from the abuse. It was relentless. When he was finally removed from the home he was nothing but a silent shell. When he began coming to art therapy

Figure 49   *An initial drawing.*

sessions he sat huddled in the chair, frightened like a beaten animal. Eventually, he learned my office was safe. He noticed the art materials. He began to draw. Jake never said much in the beginning. He let the art speak for him (Figure 49). Jake's initial drawings were catalysts for discussions about his past. Jake could not get enough of art making in one session. His projects grew and were carried over from session to session. Projects, such as a birdhouse, took many weeks to complete. He proudly brought these masterpieces back to the residential home (Figure 50). His peers complimented him. He was somebody with a talent. He had so much to share. Jake began to recognize his potential through art. He was no longer a failure, a "retard," a disgrace. He knew he was worthy. Jake broke out of his shell. He wants to be an artist.

I encourage all those who work with people who have been abused to explore and utilize alternatives to traditional talk therapy, especially for those who have a disability. Their trauma is as painful as the next person. Do not perpetuate the abuse by denying opportunities to heal. Our memories, dreams, and nightmares are not formed in words, but in visual pictures. To release these, it will take more than a thousand words. Silence is no longer necessary. Creative expression is a liberating ex-

96

perience. It is a magical and powerful gift to which all are entitled. It only takes one person to believe in humanity for all. One person can provide the love, understanding, and support to make all the difference in the world.

Could that one person be you?

Figure 50   *Pride is reflected in this nurturing home.*

Aiello, D. (1984-1986). Issues and concerns confronting disabled assault victims: Strategies for treatment and prevention. *Sexuality and Disability*, 7(3/4), 96-101.

Baladerian, N.J., et al. (1986). *Survivor: For people with developmental disabilities who have been sexually assaulted. Booklet 1: For those who read best with few words.* Los Angeles, CA: Los Angeles Commission on Assaults Against Women (ERIC Document Reproduction Service No. ED 292 263).

Bartlette, D. (Fall, 1992). Child Abuse and Developmental Disabilities. *Virginia Child Protection Newsletter*, Vol. 37.

Courtois, C. (1988). *Healing the Incest Wound.* New York, London: W.W. Norton & Company.

Federation, S.(1986). Treatment Modalities for the Younger Child-Sexual Abuse. *Journal of Psychosocial Nursing*, 24(7:21).

Freeman, L. & Deach, C. (1986). *Loving Touches: A book for children about positive, caring kinds of touching.* WA: Parenting Press, Inc.

Freeman, L. & Deach, C. (1986). *It's My Body.* WA: Parenting Press, Inc.

Garbarino, J., Brookhauser, P., Authier, K., & Associates. (1987). *Special Children-Special Risks: The Maltreatment of Children with Disabilities.* New York: Aldine De Gruyter.

Henley, D. (1992). *Exceptional Children, Exceptional Art.* Massachusetts: Davis Publications, Inc.

Herman, J.L. (1992). *Trauma and Recovery.* New York: Basic Books.

Hindman, J. (1983). *A Very Touching Book...for little people and for big people*. Oregon: McClure-Hindman Associates.

Hingsburger, D. (1991). *I Witness: History and a person with developmental disability*. Mountville: VIDA Publishing.

Hingsburger, D. (1995). *Just Say Know! Understanding and reducing the risks of sexual victimization of people with developmental disabilities*. Eastman, Quebec: Diverse City Press, Inc.

James, B. (1989). *Treating Traumatized Children: New insights and creative interventions*. Massachusetts: Lexington Books.

Kramer, E. (1971). *Arts as Therapy with Children*. New York: Schocken Press.

Lowenfeld, V. (1961). *Creative and Mental Growth*. New York: The MacMillan Company.

Malchiodi, C. (1990). *Breaking the Silence: Art therapy with children from violent homes*. New York: Schocken Press.

Miller, A. (1990). *The Untouched Key: Tracing childhood trauma in creativity and destructiveness*. New York: Anchor Books, Doubleday.

Rayner, C. (1979). *The Body Book*. London: Pan Books.

Rubin, J. (1984). *The Art of Art Therapy*. New York: Brunner/Mazel.

Serrano, J. (1989). The arts in therapy with survivors of incest. *Advances in Art Therapy*. New York: John Wiley & Sons.

Sgroi, S. (1989). *Vulnerable Populations: Sexual abuse treatment for children, adult survivors, offenders and persons with mental retardation. 2*. Lexington, MA: Lexington Books.

Silver, R. (1978). *Developing Cognitive and Creative Skills Through Art*. University Park Press.

Simonds, S. (1994). *Bridging the Silence: Nonverbal modalities in the treatment of adult survivors of childhood sexual abuse.* New York: W.W. Norton & Company, Inc.

Sobsey, D. (1990). *Annotated Bibliography: Disability, sexuality and abuse.* Baltimore: Paul H. Brookes.

Sobsey, D. (1992). What We Know About Abuse and Disabilities. *NRCCSA News*, Vol.1, NO.4, Nov./Dec.

Sobsey, D. (1994). *Violence and Abuse in the Lives of People with Disabilities: The end of silent acceptance?* Baltimore: Paul H. Brookes.

Sobsey, D. (1995). *Violence & Disability: An annotated bibliography.* Baltimore: Paul H. Brookes.

Sweet, P.E. (1981). *Something Happened to Me.* WI: Mother Courage Press.

Tobin, P. (1992). Addressing special vulnerabilities in prevention. *NRCCSA News*, 1(4) Nov./Dec.

Vanderbilt, H. (1992). Incest: A chilling report, *Lear's*, February.

Wilson, L. (1977). Theory and practice of art therapy with the mentally retarded. *American Journal of Art Therapy.* 16, 87-97.

Wisechild, L. & Randall, M (1991). *She Who Was Lost is Remembered: Healing from incest through creativity.* Washington: The Seal Press.

About Diverse City Press   (514) 297-3080

Diverse City Press has set a goal of publishing vital, insightful, yet affordable material for people in the field of developmental disabilities. We are open to comments regarding our books and videos, we are also open to receiving manuscripts from individuals who work directly with people with developmental disabilities.

Other Products Available

The Psychiatric Tower of Babble: Understanding People with Developmental Disabilities who have Mental Illness, by Sue Gabriel

Just Say Know! Understanding and Reducing the Risk of Sexual Victimization of People With Developmental Disabilities, by Dave Hingsburger

Hand Made Love: Teaching about Male Masturbation through Understanding and Video, by Dave Hingsburger

Under Cover Dick: Teaching about Condom Use through Understanding and Video, by Dave Hingsburger

Behaviour Self! Using Behavioural Concepts to Understand and Work with People with Developmental Disabilities, by Dave Hingsburger

No How! An Instructional Tape By People With Disabilities For People With Disabilities About Stopping Abuse

About the Author

Cynthia Caprio-Orsini, MA, A.T.R., a registered art psychotherapist, specializes in working with trauma survivors. Ms. Caprio-Orsini has presented throughout Canada and the Northeast on the topic of art therapy and trauma as it relates to various populations. She is a member of the International Society for the Study for Training and Development. She is a partner of **The Forum: Advancement of Trauma Education**, providing educational support to professionals treating trauma. Ms. Caprio-Orsini maintains a private practice in Rochester, New York and consults for area agencies.

About the Artist

Leoma Thomas is an artist with a developmental disability. She is and very kind and giving person with a great sense of humor.

Leoma has been employed for about a year. She is a very diligent worker and enjoys all types of art work.

Picture from the private collection of Diverse City Press, Inc.

Mouth: the voice of disability rights

"Mouth is an angry, in your face, bitchy, funny magazine that provokes, informs and inspires. It takes societal attitudes and holds them up to the harsh light of day. People with disabilities will find community, professionals will find challenge. This magazine is a *must* subscription." Dave Hingsburger

Subscription rates:

US $16 person with disability $48 agency

Mouth
61 Brighton Street
Rochester, NY
14607